The *The* **DONUT DADDY** COOKBOOK

TEN SPEED PRESS
California | New York

The

DONUT DADDY COOKBOOK

SUGAR & SEDUCTION IN 69 RECIPES

ANTHONY RANDELLO-JAHN
& RALUCA TIGANILA

PHOTOGRAPHY BY
ANTHONY RANDELLO-JAHN
& HANNAH CALDWELL

Contents

01

Donuts Dipped in Desire 23

02

Mix and Chill 77

Introduction

Hey there, dessert lovers.

I was born Anthony Randello-Jahn, but you can call me the Donut Daddy. Welcome to my world. Nestled in the heart of Melbourne, where the aroma of freshly brewed coffee mingles with the sweet scent of indulgence, lies my sanctuary, a haven for anyone with a sweet tooth.

But I have a confession to make. Lean a little closer and I'll whisper it in your ear: I wasn't always the donut master you see today. My journey began in a humble kitchen, where I taught myself the alchemy of baking. It was there, amid the clouds of flour and vanilla, that I discovered my passion for crafting sweets. I became mesmerized by the delicate balance of flavors and the intricate designs of desserts. I would knead and caress the dough, I would delicately shape my creations, I would watch them with anticipation as they baked in the oven. It was not just a passion, it was a calling.

Determined to revolutionize the everyday donut, I threw myself into studying, experimenting, and perfecting my craft. I blended traditional techniques with innovative twists, creating donuts that weren't just delicious but were true masterpieces. Each one tells a story of inspiration, passion, and a touch of whimsy. And the world became enraptured with my creations, sneaking off to enjoy them in private whenever they could.

As my fame grew, I wanted to share my art in a more intimate and engaging way. That's when I turned to the digital stage, creating sensual and stunning videos to showcase the beauty and bounty of my innermost desire: desserts. My videos are not tutorials—they are an invitation to explore the sensory delights of baking, teasing not only your palate but your imagination as well.

The name "Donut Daddy" is a title I wear seriously and with pride. It reflects not just my mastery over donuts but my role as a guide, leading you into a world where pleasure and artistry converge. My leap to this new identity has been transformative, allowing me to reach a wider audience and share my passion with the world. Now, I am the proud owner of Levain Donuts in Melbourne. It's here that I constantly create new types of donuts and present them to the world, continuing my journey of sweet innovation.

I'm thrilled to bring you my first cookbook, *The Donut Daddy Cookbook*. In this book, I'm baring it all and opening the doors to my kitchen to unveil my most beloved recipes, each with its own backstory, and tips to help you bring a seductive allure into your own home.

But this isn't just a cookbook. It is a manifesto for the joy of cooking and the art of indulgence. With these pages, I want to encourage you to embrace your desires, find beauty in the process, and create sensual experiences that linger long after the last bite. This book is a celebration of the senses, a tribute to the power of imagination, and a testament to the transformative magic of a simple donut.

So, let's embark on this delicious journey together. Get ready to seduce your taste buds and ignite your passion for baking. Step into the world of the Donut Daddy!

How to Use This Book

Is it your first time . . . baking? Don't worry, I've got some tips and tricks that will help you achieve ecstatic results. And even if you've experienced the heat of the oven a few times before, the tips below will take your technique to the next level.

For heavenly results every time, use a scale to measure out your dry ingredients. But if you insist on being naughty, I've got you covered with cup and tablespoon measurements.

When baking, one of the first steps to ensure accuracy is to invest in a good digital kitchen scale, which can be found online for less than twenty dollars. Many modern recipes, especially those for baking, provide ingredient measurements by weight rather than volume, because weighing leads to more consistent results. You want to make sure you get what you want every time, right? Weighing ingredients like flour, sugar, or butter is the best way to do that, ensuring that you're using the exact amount needed. Cups will work, but when you scoop with the cup, you don't always pick up the same amount of flour, which can lead to discrepancies in your measurements. It's a common pitfall and one that weighing allows you to avoid. If you're more comfortable using cup measurements, make sure you understand the proper way to measure each ingredient, which means leveling off dry ingredients or using liquid measuring cups for wet ingredients. It's okay to use cups—I want you to feel comfortable in the kitchen. But familiarizing yourself with both methods will help you follow the recipes more precisely and achieve better results in your cooking.

You can find out precisely how hot it is in here by buying a thermometer. It'll allow you to check your precise oven temperature or the temperature of your ingredients when needed for certain methods, like tempering chocolate.

You don't want to get too hot too fast, right? Temperature control is crucial in cooking, and investing in a reliable kitchen thermometer can greatly enhance your results and give you a deeper understanding of the baking process. Many recipes rely on precise temperatures, and a baking thermometer can ensure that your oven is at the correct heat for baking or that you have achieved the ideal temperature for tempering chocolate. For example, candy making often requires specific temperature stages, and a thermometer can help you achieve the perfect consistency—something smooth and silky.

You deserve the very best, so as much as you can afford to, buy the best ingredients possible and be discerning in your selection. You're putting this in your mouth, after all.

Choosing the right ingredients is fundamental to the success of any recipe in a cookbook. Start by carefully reading the ingredients list and instructions to understand what's required. Pay attention to specific details, like whether the recipe calls for fresh fruits versus dried, or if certain ingredients need to be at room temperature. The quality of your ingredients can significantly affect the final dish, so whenever possible, opt for fresh, high-quality products.

HOW TO WEIGH INGREDIENTS USING A SCALE

1 Place your digital scale on a flat, stable surface. Turn it on and ensure it's set to the correct unit of measurement (grams, ounces, etc.) specified in your recipe.

2 Place an empty bowl or container on the scale, then press the "tare" or "zero" button. This resets the scale to zero, so the weight of the container is not included in the measurement of your ingredients.

3 Add the ingredient to the container slowly, watching the display on the scale as you add and reach the desired weight. If the recipe calls for multiple ingredients to be combined, you can press "tare" after each ingredient to reset the scale before adding the required amount for the next.

HOW TO MEASURE DRY INGREDIENTS USING CUPS

1 **Choose the right cup:** When I'm baking, I always reach for a dry measuring cup specifically designed for ingredients like flour, sugar, or cocoa powder. These cups are great because you can fill them right to the brim and then easily level off the excess, which makes a big difference in getting the right amount of each ingredient.

2 **Leveling is key:** I have learned over time that one of the most important steps is leveling off the top of the cup after you have filled it. I usually grab the back of a butter knife and gently sweep it across the top of the cup. This simple trick helps ensure that I'm not accidentally using too much or too little of an ingredient, which could throw off the entire recipe.

3 **No packing, unless asked for:** I cannot stress enough how important it is not to pack down ingredients like flour unless the recipe specifically says to do so. I used to make this mistake, and it always resulted in a heavier, denser baked good than I wanted. Just lightly scoop and level off—your donuts will thank you!

4 **Handle sugar with care:** When it comes to sugar or other granular ingredients, I've found that it's best to just scoop or pour it into the measuring cup without pressing it down before leveling it off. If the recipe calls for something like packed brown sugar, I give it a gentle press into the cup until it's nicely compacted and then level it off. This ensures I'm getting just the right sweetness in every bite.

HOW TO MEASURE LIQUID INGREDIENTS USING CUPS

1 **Use the right measuring cup:** When it comes to liquids like water, milk, or juice, I always use a liquid measuring cup, which is designed with a spout for easy pouring and has measurements marked on the side. This type of cup makes it easy to get an accurate read at eye level, discussed below.

2 **Check at eye level:** One thing I've learned is to always double-check the measurement by getting down to eye level with the cup. This way, whether I'm measuring oil for a cake or cream for a mousse, I know I'm not accidentally adding too much or too little.

3 **Measure carefully:** For thicker liquids like cream or oil, I pour slowly to avoid overshooting the measurement. With oil, I especially take my time, as it can be a bit trickier to pour. If I'm ever unsure, I just take a moment to let it settle in the cup before rechecking the amount.

4 **Avoid spills and waste:** One tip I like to use, especially when pouring small amounts of liquid into measuring spoons, is to pour over a bowl. This way, if I accidentally pour too much, I can easily transfer it back without making a mess or wasting ingredients.

Basic Ingredients and Equipment

I like to keep a stocked pantry so I can follow my whims when I'm in the kitchen. Do I want a light and dreamy dessert? Or an indulgent and creamy creation? If I've got the ingredients that follow on hand, I can make whatever I desire whenever I desire it. Included are some of my favorite brands to work with.

BASIC INGREDIENTS

- **Baking powder:** Arm & Hammer Baking Powder

- **Baking soda:** Arm & Hammer Baking Soda

- **Bittersweet chocolate:** Valrhona Guanaja Chocolate Fèves (70% cacao)

- **Bread flour:** King Arthur Baking Company Unbleached Bread Flour

- **Butter:** Président Butter (Unsalted)

- **Cocoa powder:** Navitas Organics Organic Cacao Powder

- **Cornstarch:** Bob's Red Mill Cornstarch

- **Couverture:** Callebaut Couverture Chocolate (54.5% Belgian Dark Chocolate)

- **Cream:** Organic Valley Organic Heavy Whipping Cream (35%)

- **Dough improver:** King Arthur Baking Company Whole Grain Dough Improver

- **Eggs:** Vital Farms Organic Eggs

- **Filtered water:** Any filtered water or purified water

- **Flour:** King Arthur Baking Company Unbleached All-Purpose Flour

- **Gelatin sheets:** gold, silver, or platinum strength like Dr. Oetker Leaf Gelatine (Gold Strength)

- **Gelatin powder:** Knox Unflavored Gelatin

- **Granulated, caster, confectioners', brown, and superfine sugars:** Wholesome

- **Milk chocolate:** Ghirardelli Milk Chocolate Premium Baking Chips

- **Semisweet chocolate:** Guittard Semisweet Chocolate Baking Chips

- **Unsweetened dark chocolate:** Baker's Unsweetened Chocolate Baking Bar

- **Vanilla bean paste:** Nielsen-Massey Madagascar Bourbon Pure Vanilla Bean Paste

- **Vanilla essence:** Nielsen-Massey Madagascar Bourbon Pure Vanilla Extract

- **Vegetable oil:** 365 Whole Foods Market Vegetable Oil

- **Vegetable shortening:** Crisco All-Vegetable Shortening or Nutiva Organic Shortening

- **White chocolate:** Callebaut White Chocolate Couverture (28% cacao)

- **Whole milk:** Maple Hill Organic Whole Milk

- **Yeast:** Red Star Active Dry Yeast

DONUT DADDY'S SECRET ARSENAL (EQUIPMENT)

Welcome to the heart of the operation, the tools that turn simple ingredients into moments of pure indulgence. In my world, every piece of equipment has a role to play, from the essentials that no dessert artist should be without to the luxurious extras that bring a little bit of flair. Some tools are essential, the bare necessities that make every recipe a reality. Others are nice-to-haves, the kinds of things that make your process smoother and your final product shine. And finally, there are the specialized tools, those unique, almost indulgent pieces of equipment that add a touch of alchemy when the ordinary just won't do.

Essential Equipment: The Bare Minimum for Maximum Pleasure

These are the basics, the nonnegotiables. They're like the first dance in donut seduction. Trust me, once you have these essentials in hand, you'll be ready to turn up the heat, take control, and dive right into donut bliss.

Baking sheets: The sturdy, reliable foundation for all your creations. In American baking, a *baking sheet* typically refers to a flat, rimmed metal pan used for baking everything from cookies to roasted vegetables. If you're looking for a completely flat version with no raised edges, that would be a *cookie sheet* in U.S. terminology. Either way, these kitchen staples are ready to handle anything you throw at them, from dough to glaze.

Bowls: Mixing bowls of all sizes—because the right bowl can hold all your ingredients, your hopes, and your dreams of delicious donuts.

Measuring cups and measuring spoons: Precision is everything in the Donut Daddy domain. Every ounce, every teaspoon—because even a little too much or too little can throw the whole thing off.

Oven: The grand finale. This is where things get hot, steamy, and delicious. When it's ready, you'll know.

Plastic wrap: To cover bowls and create a warm environment for the dough to rise.

Rolling pin: Smooth, solid, and ready to roll things out to just the right thickness. This one has a firm touch, but it knows when to be gentle.

Scale: For when you want to get down to the gram. The Donut Daddy way is all about accuracy, and this little number is the key to getting it just right.

Silicone spatulas: Flexible, dependable, and know how to scrape every last bit out and leave no crumb behind.

Stand mixer with dough hook, paddle, and whisk attachments: Your hands-free partner. Powerful and reliable, it kneads, mixes, and whips without breaking a sweat.

Thermometer: Temperature control is everything—keep things warm, never too hot, just the way you want it.

Timer: Timing is everything, darling. With this, you'll hit that sweet spot every time, ensuring every rise, rest, and bake is perfectly executed.

Nice-to-Haves: The Little Luxuries

Sure, you don't need these, but life's a lot more fun when you indulge a little. These tools make things easier, fancier, and a whole lot smoother. With these in your lineup, you'll feel like the true kitchen master, crafting every dessert with a dash of style and a whole lot of flair.

Baking weights (also called pie weights) are small, heat-resistant objects used to keep pastry dough from puffing up or shrinking while blind baking. You can use ceramic or metal baking weights, or you can even use dried beans, uncooked rice, or granulated sugar as a substitute.

Cake and loaf pans: When you want to add a little height, a little heft. Donuts might be the main squeeze, but a cake or loaf? That's a whole new level of dessert seduction.

Cooling racks: Perfect for showing off your golden beauties' curves as they cool, these wire racks let your creations rest without getting soggy bottoms.

Cutting boards: Because every masterpiece deserves a solid, stable stage to begin its journey.

Damp tea towels: To cover the dough while it rests, ensuring it stays pillowy soft.

Guitar sheet: A flexible and clear plastic sheet commonly used in pastry and chocolate work. It provides a nonstick, smooth surface, making it ideal for rolling butter, laminating dough, and spreading and tempering chocolate evenly. If guitar sheets aren't available, you can use parchment paper or silicone baking mats.

Hand mixer: For those times when you want to take it easy, just a quick blend without losing control.

Large heavy pot: 5- or 6-quart for frying the donuts.

Metal spatulas: Lifting, flipping, serving with finesse. Spatulas are like gentle hands that know just where to be.

Pastry bags and tips: The essential tools for decorating, filling, and adding artistic flair to your creations. Pastry bags come in reusable silicone or disposable plastic options, with sizes ranging from small 12-inch (30-cm) bags for fine detailing to larger 18-inch (45-cm) bags for handling generous fillings. The tips vary in shape and size—round tips (like Wilton #12) are ideal for filling donuts, star tips (such as #1M) create beautiful swirls, and specialty tips can be used for intricate designs. For the best results, choose high-quality stainless-steel tips and sturdy bags that offer control and durability. These tools can be found at baking supply stores, specialty kitchen shops, or online retailers.

Pastry brush: When you need to spread that glaze, just a thin, even coat—like painting on a little extra temptation.

Serrated knife: Precision cutting for that perfect split, each slice a clean, controlled motion.

Silicone baking mats: Nonstick, smooth, and sleek, these mats make sure nothing gets stuck. Effortless cleanup, every time.

Slotted spoon: The gentle scoop for lifting the donuts from the oil without losing that perfect shape. Smooth and graceful, it knows just how to handle the heat.

Specialized Equipment: The Luxurious Extras

Now we're in the big leagues. These are the tools you don't really need, but when you've got them, they take your creations from delicious to irresistible. Think of these as the cherry on top, the tools that bring out the full Donut Daddy experience.

Chopsticks: Perfect for flipping those hot donuts without leaving a mark. Delicate yet precise, they're the unexpected heroes of the kitchen.

Culinary torch: Because sometimes you want to finish with a kiss of flame. Perfect for caramelizing or adding that final, seductive touch.

Donut cutters: For cutting out that classic, round donut shape with precision. It's all about creating that perfect circle. I recommend having a 1-inch (2.5-cm) cutter (for donut holes) and a 3-inch (7.5-cm) cutter (for the classic donut shape) on hand.

Donut pans: Essential for baked donuts, these pans create that signature donut shape while eliminating the need for frying. If you prefer a lighter option, these are your best friends.

Food processor: Smooth, creamy fillings and the finest crumbs? This powerhouse is how you get it done.

Grater: For gentle hints of citrus zest, a fine dusting of chocolate. Just a little garnish, but oh, does it make a difference.

Molds: When you're ready to get fancy with shapes. Because sometimes your decadent creations need to go above and beyond.

Muffin tins: Since some recipes call for them, they deserve a mention. Great for small cakes, muffins, and even certain baked donuts.

Parchment paper: While not exactly a luxury, it's a game-changer for easy cleanup and nonstick baking. Line trays, wrap dough, or roll out delicate pastries effortlessly.

Peeler: For those delicate curls of citrus peel or a touch of garnish that brings everything together.

Saucepans and skillets: Essential for heating cream, making caramel, and frying smaller batches of donuts. Since we're including saucepans, let's add skillets, too—they're just as useful for melting butter or toasting nuts.

Sieve: Keeps things smooth and refined, free of lumps. Only the good stuff makes it through.

Tartlet rings: These sleek rings are perfect for structured, layered desserts. Unlike traditional tart pans, these bottomless metal molds let the dough breathe, creating a perfectly structured crust that doesn't slump or shrink.

MORE TIPS

How to Fill a Donut

To fill a donut properly, start by preparing a piping bag with your desired filling, whether it's pastry cream, jam, or ganache. Fit the bag with a round piping tip between ¼ inch (6mm) and ½ inch (12mm) in diameter, such as a Wilton #230 for deep, controlled filling or a #12 round tip for general use. Once the bag is filled, twist the top to secure the filling and apply steady pressure. If the donut has a premade hole from frying or baking, gently insert the piping tip into it; if not, use a paring knife or chopstick to create a small opening on the side. Slide the tip about halfway into the donut and squeeze the bag steadily while slowly pulling the tip back. You'll feel the donut expand slightly as it fills—stop before it overflows. If needed, rotate the donut and insert the tip from another angle to ensure even distribution. A well-filled donut should feel slightly heavier and give a little when gently pressed. Wipe off any excess filling at the opening, then finish with a dusting of powdered sugar, a dip in glaze, or a drizzle of chocolate. Now, it's ready to be enjoyed.

Don't Have a Scale?

Time to get hands-on. Just trust your instincts, Donut Daddy–style. Start by dividing the dough in half, then keep cutting each piece in half again until you have fifteen or twenty portions, depending on the recipe. Aim for each one to be about the size of a golf ball, maybe a touch smaller, just enough to fill your palm with soft, pillowy promise. Roll each piece into a smooth, round ball, savoring the dough's velvety touch in your hands.

The Windowpane Test

A dough passes this test when it stretches thin enough to become slightly translucent without tearing. Aim for a thickness similar to delicate parchment paper—a sign that your dough is fully developed and ready to rise.

About Dough Improver

Dough improver is a premade dough conditioner that helps to give your dough a better rise and improve its texture using a blend of ingredients like ascorbic acid, soy lecithin, and enzymes. It's easy to use at home, and typically your dough requires just a teaspoon or so. I recommend using King Arthur Baking Company's version to create consistent results.

About Filtered Water

Filtered water is free of impurities like chlorine, which can interfere with yeast activity. In recipes that require yeast, filtered water ensures that the yeast works optimally, leading to a better rise and a softer dough that's easier to knead.

About Pectin NH

This is a specific type of pectin used in professional pastry and dessert making to aid in creating stable, smooth jellies and glazes. This pectin variation works well with acidic ingredients and provides a desirable gel-like texture, making it perfect for inserts like the cherry jelly insert on page 151. It needs to be cooked to activate its gelling properties. Combining it with sugar before adding it to the liquid helps prevent clumping. A common brand is Louis François Pectin NH. Powdered pectin such as Sure-Jell is a substitute.

About Bread Flour

Bread flour has a higher protein content (12% to 14%) than "regular" flour (8% to 11%), which creates more gluten for structure and chew, perfect for bread and donuts that need a strong rise and a light, airy texture. If you don't have bread flour, King Arthur Baking Company All-Purpose Flour (with its higher-than-average 11.7% protein content) works beautifully for donuts. It's strong enough to deliver a great rise while keeping your donuts tender and soft.

About Fléchard Butter Sheets

These are high-quality, professional-grade laminated butter sheets typically used in pastry making when a recipe calls for "laminating" a dough, or repeatedly folding and rolling sheets of butter into a dough to create buttery, airy layers. They are specially designed for laminated doughs like those for croissants, puff pastry, and Danish pastries. The butter is crafted to have a high fat content, usually around 82%, which is ideal for creating layers in laminated dough.

Gelatin 101: Sheets vs. Powder

Gelatin is what gives desserts like panna cotta their signature silky wobble. It comes in two forms: sheets and powdered gelatin. Gelatin sheets are measured by weight and bloom strength (gold, silver, platinum). The higher the bloom, the firmer the set. Gold is the most commonly used in pastry. Powdered gelatin needs to be "bloomed" in cold water before using (about 1 teaspoon powder per ½ cup of liquid). When substituting, 1 sheet of gold gelatin equals approximately ½ teaspoon of powdered gelatin.

What Is Couverture Chocolate?

Couverture chocolate is a high-quality chocolate with a higher percentage of cocoa butter (at least 31%), making it ideal for tempering, melting, and creating silky-smooth desserts. Unlike regular chocolate, couverture melts more fluidly, resulting in a glossy finish and rich mouthfeel—perfect for ganache, soufflés, and glazes.

Donuts Dipped
in Desire

A Naughty, Glazed Affair

Well, well, well . . . welcome to the playground, sugar! In this chapter, the dough gets hot and heavy, cream knows exactly where it needs to go, and every glaze drips with pure temptation. These are not your average donuts—no, baby—these are love letters written in sugar, fried in oil, and dipped into everything your wildest cravings ever dreamed of. You'll find that every donut here is a little sinful, a little seductive, and guaranteed to leave you begging for one more bite.

You already know the drill: I'm the Donut Daddy, and I know what you knead. Around here, we don't just roll dough, we romance it. We slap it, pinch it, stretch it, and let it rise until it can't take it anymore. We don't simply fry—we transform, creating sweet sensations. Watch that dough puff up in the heat, turning golden and glistening—trust me, it knows exactly what it's doing.

Listen! The recipes that follow are not just donuts. They are moments of pure pleasure, wrapped in sugar and fried to perfection. Whether you are eating them on the couch, in bed, or . . . well, wherever you like to indulge, these donut recipes are here to satisfy every indulgence. And the best part? You can do it all yourself . . . but don't worry; Daddy will be right there with you. And don't forget to live in the moment: All of these fried delights are best enjoyed the day of, freshly glazed and warm to the touch.

So, roll out that dough, heat the oil, and let's get messy!

As the sun barely peeks over the horizon, you step into your kitchen, ready to work your magic. You've entered my domain, the domain of the Donut Daddy. Your hands dive into the soft dough, feeling it come to life under your touch, warm and pliable, like it is made just for you. You know the soft dough will need to withstand the heat of the fryer, for that is the Donut Daddy way. Get ready for the first bite, as it will be pure ecstasy and a moment of sweet indulgent satisfaction. When people see the glow on your face they will know: You mastered the art of being your own Donut Daddy.

Hot Glazed Ring Donuts

MAKES 20 DONUTS

FOR THE DONUTS

4 cups (560g) bread flour

¼ cup (50g) granulated sugar

¾ teaspoon kosher salt

2 teaspoons active dry yeast

1 teaspoon dough improver (see page 20; optional)

1⅔ cups (395ml) filtered water (see page 20), at room temperature

¼ cup (55g) unsalted butter or vegetable shortening, cubed

Vegetable oil for frying (about 5 quarts [4.8L], depending on pot size)

FOR THE GLAZE

4¾ cups (570g) confectioners' sugar

Seeds from 1 vanilla bean

½ cup (120ml) hot water

MAKE THE DONUTS

In the bowl of a stand mixer, let your fingers fall into the bread flour, granulated sugar, salt, yeast, and dough improver (if using), mixing them together with a gentle touch of your fingertips until they are intimately combined. Feel free to start this step with your hands to get a tactile sense of the ingredients, but then switch to the paddle attachment on your stand mixer on low speed to bring everything together thoroughly. This initial blend should be gentle, keeping the ingredients light and airy.

Slowly, seductively, pour the filtered water into the mix while the mixer continues on low speed. Feel the transformation as the ingredients unite into a silky dough. Once the water is mostly absorbed, begin adding the butter in small pieces. The fat should be added when the dough is already forming but still feels slightly sticky and soft, giving you a satiny feel under your fingers. The texture should be smooth and supple before adding the fat, but not too dry. Mix on medium speed until everything is well incorporated, about 3 minutes.

As the dough begins to take shape, switch to the dough hook. Knead the dough with passion and care on medium speed until it becomes as smooth and elastic as the most tender embrace, 10 to 15 minutes. Keep the dough's temperature below 84°F (29°C) (check the temperature by inserting a thermometer's probe into the center of the dough), ensuring it remains warm but

CONTINUED

Hot Glazed Ring Donuts

not too hot, just like the touch of a lover's hand. Test it by stretching a small piece between your fingers, teasing it into a delicate windowpane (see page 20).

Grease a large bowl and transfer this tender dough to the bowl. Cover the bowl with plastic wrap and let the dough rise in a warm, inviting place until it swells to twice its size, full and round, 1 hour.

Lightly flour a baking sheet and set aside. On a lightly floured surface, gently roll out the risen dough to a thickness of ½ inch (1.3cm). Use a 3-inch (7.5-cm) round donut cutter for the classic ring shape and a smaller 1-inch (2.5-cm) cutter for the hole, creating the familiar, seductive ring. Caress the dough with your hands as you cut out the donut shapes, placing each one on the prepared baking sheet, like delicate jewels on display. Each donut should be round and slightly soft to the touch.

Cover the donuts with a damp tea towel and let them rest in the quiet warmth for another 30 minutes. Watch as they slowly rise, becoming soft, pillowy, and ready to be transformed.

In a large heavy pot, heat the oil to 350°F (175°C). Test the oil's readiness with a small piece of dough. The dough should sizzle seductively and rise to the surface, beckoning you to begin.

Gently lower the donuts one by one, frying in batches to avoid overcrowding. Fry three or four donuts at a time, ensuring they have enough space to float and cook evenly. Watch as they dance and turn golden brown in the heat, 1 to 2 minutes per side. Use large chopsticks or tongs to carefully flip them, savoring the sight of their transformation.

Lift the donuts from the oil with a slotted spoon or tongs and place on a wire rack to cool, their warm, golden bodies tempting you with their scent. While the donuts cool, prepare the glaze.

MAKE THE GLAZE

In a medium bowl, combine the confectioners' sugar and vanilla bean seeds, letting the exotic scent of vanilla fill the air. Gradually add the hot water, stirring slowly, sensuously, until the glaze is smooth and glossy, like liquid silk.

ASSEMBLE THE HOT GLAZED RING DONUTS

While the donuts are still warm, dip them into the glaze, coating each one evenly. Place the glazed donuts back on the wire rack, watching as the glaze sets into a shiny, irresistible shell. Indulge in their sweet seduction the day of.

Watching someone bite into one of these Jam and Cream Splits you see the stages of ecstasy: the eyes rolling back in the head, the quiver on the lips, the deep sigh of satisfaction. The crisp outer layer gives way to the soft, creamy center, popping with a sweet surprise burst of raspberry jam. When you see that face, you will know that I delivered again! These are not just donuts, they are a moment of pure indulgence, crafted by your hands for the pleasure of those lucky enough to taste them.

Jam and Cream Splits

MAKES 15 DONUT SPLITS

FOR THE DONUTS

4 cups (560g) bread flour

¼ cup (30g) granulated sugar

¾ teaspoon kosher salt

2 teaspoons active dry yeast

1 teaspoon dough improver (see page 20; optional)

1⅔ cups (395ml) filtered water (see page 20), at room temperature

¼ cup (55g) unsalted butter or vegetable shortening, cubed

Vegetable oil for frying (about 5 quarts [4.8L], depending on pot size)

FOR THE CREAM

1⅔ cups (395ml) heavy cream

¼ cup (50g) superfine or caster sugar

2 teaspoons vanilla bean paste

Raspberry jam for garnish

Maraschino cherries for garnish

MAKE THE DONUTS

In the bowl of a stand mixer, let your fingers graze over the bread flour, granulated sugar, salt, yeast, and dough improver (if using). Mix them together with a gentle touch, as if coaxing them to life. Use the dough hook and set your mixer to low speed. Allow the mixer to run for 1 to 2 minutes, watching as the ingredients blend, light and airy. The mixture should feel like soft sand beneath your fingers, evenly combined and ready for what's next.

Keeping the mixer on low speed, slowly pour in the water, letting it flow like liquid silk into the flour mixture. Continue mixing until most of the water has been absorbed, 2 to 3 minutes. Introduce the cubed butter, allowing it to melt into the dough like a tender caress. The dough will start to come together, transforming from slightly sticky to smooth and cohesive. You're looking for a soft, elastic dough.

Now it's time to dig deep and knead with passion! Increase the mixer speed to medium and knead the dough until it is smooth and supple, and feels warm under your touch but never too hot, 10 to 15 minutes. Keep the dough's temperature below 79°F (26°C). Test it by stretching a small piece between your fingers, teasing it into a delicate windowpane (see page 20).

Grease a large bowl and transfer the dough to the bowl. Cover the bowl with plastic wrap and let the dough rest in a warm, quiet place, watching it rise as if it is breathing in anticipation, 1 hour.

CONTINUED

Jam and Cream Splits

CONTINUED

Lightly flour a baking sheet and set aside. Separate the rested dough into fifteen smooth, 2½-ounce (75-g) portions, rolling them into soft, round balls. Each one should feel like a promise in your hands, full of potential. If you don't have a scale, you're in big trouble. Just kidding, see Don't Have a Scale? on page 20.

Gently place the dough balls on the prepared sheet, leaving enough space for them to grow. Cover with a damp tea towel and let the balls rest for another 30 minutes to 1 hour, allowing them to swell with the anticipation of what is to come.

In a large heavy pot, heat the oil to 350°F (175°C). Depending on the size of your pot, fry three or four donuts at a time, ensuring they have enough space to float and cook evenly. As you lower the donuts into the hot oil, listen to them sizzle with excitement, turning a perfect golden brown, 1 to 2 minutes per side. Use large chopsticks or tongs to flip them, ensuring each side gets equal attention.

Lift the donuts from the oil with a slotted spoon or tongs and place them on a wire rack to cool, their warm, golden bodies waiting to be filled with something irresistible.

MAKE THE CREAM

In the bowl of a stand mixer, whisk the cream, superfine sugar, and vanilla bean paste until semifirm peaks form—creamy, luscious, and ready to be piped.

Fill a piping bag fitted with a star tip with the whipped cream, feeling the weight of it in your hands as you prepare to fill each donut with indulgence.

ASSEMBLE THE JAM AND CREAM SPLITS

Gently split each donut horizontally in two across the top, using a serrated knife. Be careful not to cut all the way through, but just enough to create a pocket of pleasure for the cream.

Pipe the cream into each donut in a smooth, circular motion, letting the cream swirl into every crevice, soft and inviting.

Add a dollop of your favorite raspberry jam on top of the cream, the sweetness contrasting beautifully with the rich cream, and finish each donut with a maraschino cherry, a final seductive touch. Enjoy the splits hot and fresh the day of.

"So, you think you can handle the thrill of the Sweet Sin Cruller, huh?" I smirk, leaning back with a glint in my eye. "These aren't just pastries, babe. They're everything you crave wrapped in buttery, cinnamon sugar bliss." I'm sure you smirk right back: "Oh, I can handle anything Donut Daddy's got cooking!" I raise an eyebrow, lean in, and whisper in your ear: "Then get ready. We are about to turn up the heat!" And just like that, we're off, flour flying, butter melting, and a sprinkle of sugar making it all worth the ride.

Sweet Sin Crullers

MAKES 12 CRULLERS

FOR THE CRULLERS

½ cup (120ml) whole milk

½ cup (120ml) water

½ cup (110g) unsalted butter

1 cup and 2 tablespoons (220g) sugar

2 teaspoons kosher salt

2 cups (280g) all-purpose flour

8 eggs, at room temperature

2 teaspoons ground cinnamon

Vegetable oil for frying (about 5 quarts [4.8L], depending on pot size)

MAKE THE CRULLERS

In a large saucepan, combine the milk, water, butter, 2 tablespoons of sugar, and salt and bring to a gentle boil, stirring just enough to watch the butter dissolve and fill the air with buttery steam. Take in the sweet aroma—it's as irresistible as the anticipation that's building.

Turn off the heat. With a bold flick of your wrist, add the flour all at once and stir vigorously. Feel the resistance as the dough thickens, coming together like destiny itself.

Turn the heat back on to medium and keep stirring for 2 to 3 minutes. The dough will become a smooth, thick mass, firm yet yielding. Think of it as the perfect embrace.

Take the pan off the heat, transfer the dough to the bowl of a stand mixer, and let the dough cool for just a few minutes. Not too much, though—you want it warm enough to welcome the eggs without cooking them.

Using the paddle attachment, start the mixer on medium speed, adding one egg at a time and letting each egg blend in fully before adding the next, 8 to 10 minutes total. Watch as your dough transforms into something shiny and glossy, full of promise.

Place the dough in a bowl, cover with plastic wrap pressed directly onto the surface of the dough, and chill in the refrigerator for at least an hour or, if you're a master of self-control, overnight.

CONTINUED

Sweet Sin Crullers

CONTINUED

In a shallow mixing bowl, stir together the remaining 1 cup (200g) of sugar and the cinnamon.

In a large heavy pot, heat the oil to 350°F (180°C). Cut parchment paper into small, individual 4 by 4-inch (10 by 10-cm) squares.

While the oil is heating, fill a piping bag fitted with a star tip (#6B or #8B) with the dough. Pipe 3-inch (7.5-cm) circles onto the prepared parchment squares—each loop a little more tantalizing than the last.

With the oil shimmering, gently lower a cruller, parchment-side up, into the hot oil, frying two to three at a time. The paper will soon curl away; use tongs to remove it, then let each cruller sizzle and turn a rich, golden brown.

Fry each side for about 5 minutes, giving them a final flip with chopsticks or tongs for that perfect crisp. Remove with a slotted spoon. Once out of the oil, toss each cruller in the cinnamon sugar while still hot and set it on a wire rack to cool just a little.

Serve these crullers warm, so the sugar melts on your lips.

"Do you remember your first kiss?" I ask, my gaze meeting yours. You pause, feeling a warm blush creeping up, and I lean in closer. "Well, get ready for the first taste that'll top it!" Lemon zest and blueberries collide in this playful yet passionate dance of flavors, all wrapped in a soft, tender bite that melts delightfully on your tongue. Sweet enough to make you weak, tangy enough to keep you coming back. Note that if you'd like to make this particular recipe gluten-free, replace the all-purpose flour with a 1:1 ratio of a gluten-free flour blend like Namaste Perfect Flour Blend.

GLUTEN-FREE OPTION

Blueberry Bliss and Lemon Kiss Donuts

MAKES 12 DONUTS

FOR THE DONUTS

¼ cup (55g) unsalted butter, melted

¼ cup (60ml) vegetable oil

¾ cup (150g) granulated sugar

2 eggs

2 teaspoons pure vanilla extract

Zest of 1 lemon

1 cup (240ml) buttermilk or whole milk

2¾ cups (385g) all-purpose flour

1½ teaspoons baking powder

½ teaspoon kosher salt

1 cup (140g) fresh blueberries

FOR THE BLUEBERRY AND LEMON GLAZE

¼ cup (35g) fresh blueberries, plus more for garnish

1 tablespoon warm water

Juice of ½ lemon

4¾ cups (570g) confectioners' sugar

MAKE THE DONUTS

Preheat the oven to 425°F (220°C). Prepare your tools by lightly greasing two donut pans with butter or nonstick spray.

In a large bowl, combine the melted butter, oil, and granulated sugar and whisk together. Watch as the mixture turns smooth and fluffy, like the beginning of something sweet and special. Whisk in the eggs, vanilla, lemon zest, and buttermilk until smooth and velvety, with the scent of citrus teasing your senses.

Add the flour, baking powder, and salt, folding it all together until just combined. Gently stir in the blueberries, embracing the burst of color and flavor they bring to the thick, luscious batter.

Spoon the batter into a piping bag fitted with a large round piping tip (Wilton #1A), your hands feeling the soft weight of it as you guide it toward the donut pans. Pipe the batter into each cavity, filling it halfway, just enough to promise something irresistible.

CONTINUED

Blueberry Bliss and Lemon Kiss Donuts

CONTINUED

Slide the donut pans into the hot oven, letting the heat bring them to life. Bake until the donuts rise and turn golden, and their centers are soft and perfectly set, 7 to 8 minutes. Lean back and take in the first hints of lemon and blueberries that will soon fill the kitchen with sweet and inviting scents.

Let the donuts cool in the pan for 10 minutes before transferring them to a wire rack. As they cool, you can already imagine their tender crumb beneath the glaze.

MAKE THE BLUEBERRY AND LEMON GLAZE

In a small saucepan, combine the blueberries and water and gently heat on medium-low heat until the blueberries soften and release their vibrant juices, transforming into a rich sweet syrup, 5 to 7 minutes. Add in the lemon juice and stir until smooth. Take the pan off the heat and strain the mixture into a medium bowl to remove any seeds or pulp, leaving you with a silky, deep purple elixir.

Slowly whisk the confectioners' sugar into the warm blueberry-lemon mixture. Feel the smoothness develop under your whisk, adjusting the consistency with a bit more confectioners' sugar if too thin, or a touch of water if too thick. The glaze should be glossy, thick, and ready to coat your creations.

ASSEMBLE THE BLUEBERRY BLISS AND LEMON KISS DONUTS

Dip the top of each cooled donut into the glaze, allowing the mixture to cling to every curve before dripping slowly back into the bowl. Place the glazed donuts on a wire rack to set, watching as they shine with a tempting, irresistible sheen. Dot each donut with a couple extra fresh blueberries.

Serve these donuts while they're still fresh, every bite a burst of summer's sweetness and tang.

You know, I woke up thinking about you biting into these beauties. Golden on the outside, soft and nutmeg-kissed inside, and that glaze? Maple–brown butter goodness that melts on your tongue like a slow, warm sin. You laugh, but I can see the anticipation in your eyes! "Go on," I say, nudging the plate your way. "Indulge a little!"

Old–Fashioned Maple– Brown Butter Donuts

MAKES ABOUT 18 DONUTS

FOR THE DONUTS

4½ cups (540g) cake flour

1 tablespoon baking powder

2 teaspoons kosher salt

1 teaspoon ground nutmeg

¼ cup (55g) unsalted butter, at cool room temperature

1 cup (200g) granulated sugar

4 egg yolks

1 cup (240g) sour cream

Vegetable oil for frying (about 5 quarts [4.8L], depending on pot size)

FOR THE MAPLE–BROWN BUTTER GLAZE

¾ cup (165g) unsalted butter

8 cups (900g) confectioners' sugar, sifted

2 teaspoons pure vanilla extract

1½ cups (480g) maple syrup, preferably Grade B

MAKE THE DONUTS

In a large bowl, combine the cake flour, baking powder, salt, and nutmeg and stir until fully mixed. As you stir, let the warm scent of the spices fill the air, a promise of the deliciousness to come.

In the bowl of a stand mixer fitted with the paddle attachment, combine the butter and granulated sugar and beat on medium speed until sandy and soft. Feel the subtle resistance as you mix, knowing the magic is just beginning. Add the egg yolks, one at a time, until the mixture turns light and thick, about 5 minutes, like the first whisper of something irresistible.

Lower the speed to low and gradually add the cake flour mixture to the butter mixture, alternating with the sour cream, ending with the final bit of flour. Mix until the dough comes together, slightly sticky but smooth, 3 to 4 minutes. If the dough feels a bit too soft, add a touch more flour, taming it to the perfect texture.

After mixing, gather the dough into a ball and place it in the large bowl. Cover it tightly with plastic wrap and let it chill in the refrigerator for 1 hour. As it chills, it gains strength, readying itself for the golden transformation.

CONTINUED

Old–Fashioned Maple–Brown Butter Donuts

CONTINUED

On a lightly floured surface, roll out the chilled dough to a luxurious ½-inch (1.3-cm) thickness. Use floured cutters of any size to carve out perfect rings, feeling the cool, soft dough yield beneath your hands. If the cut dough gets too warm, give it a little time in the fridge to firm up, ensuring those rings stay crisp and defined.

In a large heavy pot, heat 2 inches of oil to 325°F (165°C). Gently lower the donuts one by one, frying in batches to avoid overcrowding. When the donuts meet the oil, they come alive with a sizzle. Fry three or four donuts at a time, ensuring they have enough space to float and cook evenly, frying them for about 2 minutes per side. Using chopsticks or tongs, turn the donuts carefully, until they reach a deep golden brown. Lift them from the oil with a slotted spoon and let them drain on a wire rack, filling the room with a warm, nutty scent. While the donuts cool, make the glaze.

MAKE THE MAPLE–BROWN BUTTER GLAZE

In a small saucepan, melt the butter over medium-high heat, watching as it deepens to a rich, amber brown, 5 to 7 minutes. The aroma alone could tempt anyone. Remove from the heat before it darkens too much, capturing that nutty, seductive flavor at its peak.

In a large bowl, combine the confectioners' sugar, warm browned butter, and vanilla. Slowly pour in the maple syrup, letting it blend smoothly. With a hand mixer, mix on high speed until the glaze is smooth, glossy, and just thick enough to coat while still being pourable, 3 to 4 minutes.

ASSEMBLE THE OLD-FASHIONED MAPLE–BROWN SUGAR DONUTS

While the donuts are still warm, dip each one into the maple–brown butter glaze. Let the glaze cling to every curve, setting into a flawless, irresistible sheen as it cools.

Serve these donuts warm, with the glaze still shining and fragrant.

Get ready, because biting into these donuts is like reliving your first kiss again and again. Soft, tender dough, a creamy vanilla center, and a dark chocolate ganache to finish. This is sweet surrender, in every single nibble.

Boston Cream Velvety Donuts

MAKES 12 TO 15 DONUTS

FOR THE DONUTS

4 cups (560g) bread flour

¼ cup (50g) sugar

¾ teaspoon kosher salt

2 teaspoons active dry yeast

1 teaspoon dough improver (see page 20; optional)

1⅔ cups (395ml) filtered water (see page 20), at room temperature

¼ cup (55g) unsalted butter or vegetable shortening, cubed

Vegetable oil for frying (about 5 quarts [4.8L], depending on pot size)

FOR THE PASTRY CREAM

2 cups (475ml) whole milk

2 teaspoons vanilla bean paste

4 egg yolks

½ cup (100g) sugar

⅓ cup (45g) cornstarch

3 tablespoons unsalted butter

1½ cups (360ml) Basic Chocolate Ganache (see page 208), warmed

Chocolate shavings or unsweetened Dutch-processed cocoa powder for garnish

MAKE THE DONUTS

In the bowl of a stand mixer fitted with the dough hook, combine the bread flour, sugar, salt, yeast, and dough improver (if using). Let the soft texture of the ingredients promise something tender and sweet.

With the mixer on low speed, slowly pour in the water, allowing it to blend gently. Gradually add the butter, piece by piece, watching as the dough comes together smoothly, until the dough is soft but cohesive, about 3 minutes.

Increase the mixer speed to medium and knead the dough until it becomes smooth and elastic, with a supple feel, 10 to 15 minutes. Test it by stretching a small piece between your fingers, teasing it into a delicate windowpane (see page 20). Remember to check that the dough's temperature remains below 84°F (29°C). The dough should be soft, stretchy, and slightly tacky.

Grease a large bowl and transfer the dough to the bowl. Cover the bowl with plastic wrap and let the dough rest in a warm, dry place until it doubles in size, 1 hour. Watch it swell, full of promise, with a tender texture beneath the surface.

Lightly flour a baking sheet. Divide the rested dough into 2½-ounce (75-g) portions. Shape each portion into a smooth, round ball and place it on the prepared baking sheet, leaving space between each one.

CONTINUED

Boston Cream Velvety Donuts

CONTINUED

Cover the dough balls with a damp tea towel and let them rest for another 30 minutes, allowing them to become soft and pillowy.

In a large heavy pot, heat 2 inches (5cm) of oil to 350°F (175°C). Gently lower the balls into the hot oil, frying two or three at a time, turning them gently with chopsticks or tongs. Fry until golden brown, 1 to 2 minutes per side. Remove with a slotted spoon and place on a wire rack to cool. The donuts should have a crisp, golden exterior and a soft, airy interior.

MAKE THE PASTRY CREAM

In a medium saucepan over medium heat, combine the milk and vanilla bean paste and heat until the milk just begins to steam. The vanilla scent fills the air, soft and sweet, like a stolen moment. Don't let the mixture boil.

In a medium bowl, whisk together the egg yolks, sugar, and cornstarch until pale and smooth. Slowly add a little of the hot milk into the egg mixture, whisking continuously, then slowly pour in the remaining milk while whisking.

Pour the mixture back into the saucepan and cook over medium heat, stirring until thickened and just beginning to boil. Continue for another 1 to 2 minutes to ensure perfect smoothness.

Remove from the heat and whisk in the butter until glossy and rich. Press plastic wrap directly onto the surface of the cream and let it cool completely.

ASSEMBLE THE BOSTON CREAM VELVETY DONUTS

Once the pastry cream and donuts have cooled, it's time to assemble your delicious treats. Fill a piping bag fitted with a #12 round tip (½-inch [13-mm]) with the pastry cream. Poke a hole in each cooled donut with a skewer and fill each one with pastry cream, feeling the soft pressure as the cream finds its way into every corner of the donut. (See page 20 for more filling tips.)

Dip the top of each filled donut into the warm chocolate ganache, letting it coat the surface in a rich, glossy layer. For the final touch, garnish with chocolate shavings or a light dusting of cocoa powder.

These donuts are best enjoyed fresh, with the chocolate still luscious and the pastry cream smooth.

I know what you're thinking . . . and yes, go ahead, savor the moment. This creation isn't just a donut. It is a sweet promise wrapped in tangy temptation, a sin waiting to happen. I can see the intrigue in your eyes. Get ready for citrusy lemon curd, delicate torched meringue . . . and, babe, that's just the beginning! This is the ultimate roller coaster of flavor—a treat that lingers, reminding you that sometimes life's sweetest pleasures are meant to be savored slowly.

Donut Daddy's Lemon Meringue Long Johns

MAKES 12 TO 15 LONG JOHNS

FOR THE LONG JOHNS

4 cups (560g) bread flour

¼ cup (50g) sugar

¾ teaspoon kosher salt

2 teaspoons active dry yeast

1 teaspoon dough improver (see page 20; optional)

1⅔ cups (395ml) filtered water (see page 20), at room temperature

¼ cup (55g) unsalted butter or vegetable shortening, cubed

Vegetable oil for frying (about 5 quarts [4.8L], depending on pot size)

FOR THE LEMON CURD

¾ cup (175ml) freshly squeezed lemon juice

¾ cup (150g) sugar

½ cup (110g) unsalted butter, cubed

3 eggs

1 tablespoon freshly grated lemon zest

FOR THE MERINGUE

9 egg whites, at room temperature

Pinch of kosher salt

2¾ cups (550g) sugar

1½ teaspoons pure vanilla extract

MAKE THE LONG JOHNS

In the bowl of a stand mixer fitted with the dough hook, combine the bread flour, sugar, salt, yeast, and dough improver (if using). With the mixer on low speed, slowly pour in the water, letting it blend smoothly. Add the butter cubes, feeling each one melt into the dough. After 2 or 3 minutes, the dough will start coming together, looking soft and cohesive.

Increase the mixer speed to medium and knead the dough, letting it develop a soft, smooth elasticity, 10 to 15 minutes. Keep the dough's temperature below 84°F (29°C), ensuring the dough stays soft, stretchy, and slightly tacky, ready for the next stage. Test it by stretching a small piece between your fingers, teasing it into a delicate windowpane (see page 20).

Grease a large bowl and transfer the dough to the bowl. Cover the bowl with plastic wrap and let the dough rest in a warm, dry place until it doubles in size, 1 hour.

Lightly flour a baking sheet and set aside. On a lightly floured surface, roll out the dough to a ½-inch (1.3-cm) thickness. Use a pizza cutter or knife to cut the dough into long rectangles,

CONTINUED

Donut Daddy's Lemon Meringue Long Johns

about 4 inches (10cm) by 1½ inches (4cm). Arrange the dough pieces on the prepared baking sheet, leaving space between each one. Cover the pieces with a damp tea towel and let them rise again until soft and pillowy, 30 minutes.

In a large heavy pot, heat the oil to 350°F (175°C). Gently lower the dough pieces into the hot oil, frying two or three at a time, until they turn a deep golden brown. Use chopsticks or tongs to turn them carefully, ensuring each side gets its golden moment, 1 to 2 minutes per side. Remove with a slotted spoon and place on a wire rack to cool.

MAKE THE LEMON CURD

In a medium saucepan, over medium heat, combine the lemon juice, sugar, and butter. Stir continuously for 2 to 3 minutes or until the sugar dissolves and the butter melts. The bright scent of citrus fills the air.

In a separate bowl, lightly beat the eggs with a whisk. Slowly add a small amount of the warm lemon mixture to the eggs, whisking continuously to temper. Gradually pour the egg mixture into the saucepan, whisking continuously. Cook over medium heat, stirring until the curd thickens and coats the back of a spoon. It should be smooth and glossy. Remove from the heat and stir in the lemon zest. Transfer the curd to a heatproof jar and let it cool completely at room temperature, uncovered. It will continue to thicken as it cools.

MAKE THE MERINGUE

Preheat the oven to 200°F (95°C). Line a baking sheet with a silicone mat.

In the bowl of a stand mixer fitted with the whisk attachment, combine the egg whites and salt and beat on medium speed for 2 to 3 minutes until soft peaks form. Increase the mixer speed to high and gradually add the sugar, beating until stiff, glossy peaks form, 10 to 15 minutes. Add the vanilla and beat briefly to combine. Reserve 3 cups of uncooked meringue for the topping.

Transfer the remaining meringue to a piping bag fitted with a #2 tip (⅛-inch or 3-mm circular tip). Pipe long, elegant sticks onto the prepared baking sheet. Bake for 10 minutes, then lower the oven temperature to 165°F (75°C) and bake until crisp, 35 to 45 minutes. Turn off the oven and let the meringue sticks cool inside the oven with the door slightly ajar for about 1 hour. Then, transfer them to a wire rack to cool completely.

ASSEMBLE THE DONUT DADDY'S LEMON MERINGUE LONG JOHNS

Fill a piping bag fitted with a ¼-inch (6-mm) tip with lemon curd and pipe it into each long john through a skewer-made hole, letting the sweet-tart filling spread throughout. Using a second piping bag with a ½-inch (1.3-cm) tip, top each donut with three or four luscious meringue dollops. Torch until golden. For a final flourish, nestle crisp meringue sticks among the peaks. Serve fresh.

Who says donuts have to be round? Welcome to the next level of indulgence: Peanut Butter Pleasure Squares! Each bite is an invitation—crunchy peanut butter glaze, a kiss of raspberry jam, and a topping of roasted peanuts. It's like a decadent love letter you'll want to sink your teeth into. Oh, I know what you knead, darlin'.

Peanut Butter Pleasure Squares

MAKES 12 TO 15 DONUT SQUARES

FOR THE DONUT SQUARES

4 cups (560g) bread flour

¼ cup (50g) sugar

¾ teaspoon kosher salt

2 teaspoons active dry yeast

1 teaspoon dough improver (see page 20; optional)

1⅔ cups (395ml) filtered water (see page 20), at room temperature

¼ cup (55g) unsalted butter or vegetable shortening, cubed

Vegetable oil for frying (about 5 quarts [4.8L], depending on pot size)

FOR THE CRUNCHY PEANUT BUTTER GLAZE

1⅔ cups (430g) crunchy peanut butter

¼ cup (45g) coarsely chopped white chocolate

1 cup (300g) raspberry jam for filling

¾ cup (90g) roasted peanuts, roughly chopped, for garnish

MAKE THE DONUT SQUARES

In the bowl of a stand mixer fitted with the dough hook, combine the bread flour, sugar, salt, yeast, and dough improver (if using). Let your fingertips feel the delicate grains, each touch building the anticipation of something rich and indulgent.

With the mixer on low speed, slowly pour in the water, watching as it seeps into the mix, a slow, tantalizing whisper. Add the cubed butter. Let the ingredients blend until the dough begins to come together, soft and pliable, yet yielding to each touch, 2 to 3 minutes.

Increase the mixer speed to medium and knead the dough, watching as it transforms into a silky, elastic mass that's slightly sticky, 10 to 15 minutes. Keep the dough's temperature below 84°F (29°C) for the perfect tender texture. Test it by stretching a small piece between your fingers, teasing it into a delicate windowpane (see page 20).

Grease a large bowl and transfer the dough to the bowl. Cover the bowl with plastic wrap and let the dough rest in a warm, dry place, swelling and filling the bowl with its soft, warm promise, 1 hour. The sight alone will tease of what's to come.

CONTINUED

Peanut Butter Pleasure Squares

Lightly flour a baking sheet and set aside. On a lightly floured surface, roll out the dough to a ½-inch (1.3-cm) thickness, feeling it yield beneath the rolling pin. Cut the dough into squares, each weighing about 2½ ounces (75g), a perfect handful of indulgence, ready to be shaped into their final form.

Place the dough squares on the prepared baking sheet, giving them space to breathe. Cover the squares with a damp tea towel and let them rest and rise until they're 1½ times their original size and feel soft and airy to the touch, another 30 to 60 minutes.

In a large heavy pot, heat the oil to 350°F (175°C). Gently lower the donut squares one by one into the hot oil, frying in batches to avoid overcrowding. Fry two or three donuts at a time, ensuring they have enough space to float and cook evenly. Watch them puff up as they sizzle and turn golden brown, 1 to 2 minutes per side. Flip them gently with chopsticks or tongs, giving each side its golden moment. Remove with a slotted spoon and place on a wire rack to cool. They'll be warm, glistening, and ready for the next layer of decadence.

MAKE THE CRUNCHY PEANUT BUTTER GLAZE

In a medium microwavable bowl, warm the peanut butter on medium at 50% power until it's loose and almost melting, 1 to 2 minutes. Stir in the white chocolate, allowing it to blend seamlessly into the peanut butter, creating a rich, creamy glaze.

ASSEMBLE THE PEANUT BUTTER PLEASURE SQUARES

Dip each donut square into the warm peanut butter glaze, coating every edge in a thick, luscious layer. Place the squares on a wire rack to let the glaze set slightly.

Fill a piping bag fitted with a #12 tip (½-inch [13-mm] circular tip) with the raspberry jam. Pierce the side of each glazed donut square with a skewer and fill the hole and top generously with jam. The sweet, tangy jam will seep into every crevice, adding a burst of flavor with each bite. Sprinkle the tops with roasted peanuts, each crunch adding a final layer of texture and indulgence.

Ah, the final touch . . . Serve these peanut butter delights while the glaze is set but still luscious, with the jam oozing out at every decadent chew. These squares don't last long—so savor every mouthful of their sweet, nutty, and jam-filled bliss.

We can do better than feeding each other basic chocolate-covered strawberries—why not make the moment much more special? These strawberry temptations are like a dance—sweet, creamy, with just the right hint of tartness. Imagine biting through soft dough, tasting the tangy strawberry glaze, and finally reaching that rich, luscious filling that oozes with every touch. Trust me, this will leave you craving more.

Strawberry Tiramisu Temptation Donuts

MAKES 12 TO 15 DONUTS

FOR THE DONUTS

4 cups (560g) bread flour

¼ cup (50g) granulated sugar

¾ teaspoon kosher salt

2 teaspoons active dry yeast

1 teaspoon dough improver (see page 20; optional)

1⅔ cups (395ml) filtered water (see page 20), at room temperature

¼ cup (55g) unsalted butter or vegetable shortening, cubed

Vegetable oil for frying (about 5 quarts [4.8L], depending on pot size)

FOR THE STRAWBERRY GLAZE

1 pound (450g) fresh or frozen strawberries

½ cup (100g) granulated sugar

1 teaspoon freshly squeezed lemon juice (optional)

6½ cups (780g) confectioners' sugar

FOR THE STRAWBERRY TIRAMISU FILLING

2 teaspoons instant coffee powder

2 cups (480g) mascarpone cheese

1¼ cups (300ml) heavy cream

1 cup (120g) confectioners' sugar

1 teaspoon pure vanilla extract

¾ cup (90g) finely chopped fresh strawberries, plus fresh strawberry halves for garnish

Freeze-dried strawberries, crushed, for garnish

MAKE THE DONUTS

In the bowl of a stand mixer fitted with the dough hook, combine the bread flour, granulated sugar, salt, yeast, and dough improver (if using). Take a moment to feel the soft, powdery mix—you're about to create something irresistible.

With the mixer on low speed, slowly pour in the water, letting it sink in like a secret. Add the butter and mix, watching as the dough begins to form, 3 minutes.

Increase the mixer speed to medium and knead the dough, feeling it warm up and come to life as it becomes soft and elastic, 10 to 15 minutes. Keep the dough's temperature below 84°F (29°C) to maintain its tender texture. Test it by stretching a small piece between your fingers, teasing it into a delicate windowpane (see page 20).

CONTINUED

Strawberry Tiramisu Temptation Donuts

Grease a large bowl and transfer the dough to the bowl. Cover the bowl with plastic wrap and let the dough rest in a warm, dry place, allowing it to rise and fill with promise, 1 hour.

Lightly flour a baking sheet and set aside. On a lightly floured surface, roll out the dough to a ½-inch (1.3-cm) thickness. Use a knife to cut the dough into squares, each weighing about 2½ ounces (75g). Each square is perfectly sized for a moment of sweet indulgence.

Place the dough squares on the prepared baking sheet, spacing them apart. Cover the squares with a damp tea towel and let them rest, allowing them to swell and soften, 30 minutes to 1 hour.

In a large heavy pot, heat the oil to 350°F (175°C). Gently lower the squares into the hot oil, frying two or three at a time, watching as they sizzle and turn golden brown, 1 to 2 minutes per side. Use chopsticks or tongs to flip them gently, ensuring a beautiful, even fry. Remove with a slotted spoon and place on a wire rack to cool.

MAKE THE STRAWBERRY GLAZE

In a small saucepan, combine the fresh strawberries, granulated sugar, and lemon juice (if using) and cook over medium-low heat until the strawberries soften and release their juices, stirring occasionally. Mash the strawberries with a fork or potato masher until they form a thick sauce. Continue cooking until the mixture reduces to a smooth, rich consistency. Reserve ⅔ cup of the mixture for the filling.

If you prefer a smoother glaze, strain the remaining strawberry mixture to remove any seeds and solid bits. Let the mixture cool slightly.

In a large bowl, combine the strawberry mixture and confectioners' sugar and mix with a wooden spoon until smooth and glossy. Set aside to cool to room temperature.

MAKE THE STRAWBERRY TIRAMISU FILLING

In a small bowl, dissolve the instant coffee in 1 to 2 tablespoons hot water. Let it cool to room temperature.

In a large mixing bowl, combine the mascarpone and the cooled coffee mixture, stirring until smooth.

In another mixing bowl, combine the cream, confectioners' sugar, and vanilla. With a hand mixer or in a stand mixer with the whisk attachment, whip the cream mixture on medium speed until stiff peaks form, 4 to 5 minutes. They should be light, fluffy, and luscious.

Gently fold the whipped cream mixture into the mascarpone mixture until fully combined. Fold in the reserved ⅔ cup of the strawberry mixture and the chopped fresh strawberries. Chill in the refrigerator to allow the filling to firm up slightly, 30 minutes.

ASSEMBLE THE STRAWBERRY TIRAMISU TEMPTATION DONUTS

Poke a hole in the top of each cooled donut with a skewer. Dip the entire donut into the strawberry glaze, letting it cling to every curve.

Pour the freeze-dried strawberries into a shallow bowl and roll the glazed donuts in them, adding color and crunch to the surface.

Fill a piping bag fitted with a large star tip with the chilled tiramisu filling. Fill each donut generously with the filling, creating soft swirls on top.

Finish by placing a fresh strawberry half on top, nestled into the creamy filling, for a final touch of elegance and flavor.

Mmm . . . Serve these beauties while the glaze is vibrant and the filling is cool and luscious. Each bite will have you wanting the next—these donuts are the perfect mix of sweet, creamy, and indulgently tangy.

So, you're ready for a little toast with Donut Daddy's Whiskey Crème Brûlée Bombs? Light the fire, cozy up, and get ready to be swept off your feet. These fiery temptations are more than simply donuts; they're warm, seductive encounters that will set your senses ablaze. Each bite gives you a soft, pillowy dough, a rich whiskey-spiked cream, and the satisfying crunch of caramelized sugar. You can thank me later.

Whiskey Crème Brûlée Bombs

MAKES 18 TO 20 DONUT BALLS

FOR THE DONUTS

4 cups (560g) bread flour

¼ cup (50g) sugar

¾ teaspoon kosher salt

2 teaspoons active dry yeast

1 teaspoon dough improver (see page 20; optional)

1⅔ cups (395ml) filtered water (see page 20), at room temperature

¼ cup (55g) unsalted butter or vegetable shortening, cubed

Vegetable oil for frying (about 5 quarts [4.8L], depending on pot size)

FOR THE WHISKEY PASTRY CREAM

2 cups (475ml) whole milk

¼ cup (60ml) whiskey

½ cup (100g) sugar

1 vanilla bean, split and seeds scraped (optional, if not using vanilla extract)

4 egg yolks

¼ cup (35g) cornstarch

2 tablespoons unsalted butter, cubed

1 teaspoon pure vanilla extract (optional, if not using a vanilla bean)

2 cups (400g) sugar for topping

Candied orange slices, homemade (see page 215) or store-bought, for garnish

MAKE THE DONUTS

In the bowl of a stand mixer fitted with the dough hook, combine the bread flour, sugar, salt, yeast, and dough improver (if using). Give it a quick mix, feeling the anticipation as the ingredients blend, building the base of something luxurious.

With the mixer on low speed, slowly pour in the water, watching it blend into the bread flour like it's sealing a promise. Add the cubed butter and mix, letting the dough come together to form a smooth and supple mass, 3 minutes.

Increase the mixer speed to medium and knead the dough, feeling it come to life as it becomes soft, elastic, and warm to the touch, 10 to 15 minutes. Keep the dough's temperature below 84°F (29°C) to maintain that perfect, tender texture. Consistency: smooth, elastic, and slightly tacky. Test it by stretching a small piece between your fingers, teasing it into a delicate windowpane (see page 20).

Grease a large bowl and transfer the dough to the bowl. Cover the bowl with plastic wrap and let the dough rest in a warm, dry place, watching it swell, doubling in size, filled with promise for what's to come, 1 hour.

CONTINUED

Whiskey Crème Brûlée Bombs

Lightly flour a baking sheet. Weigh out 2½-ounce (75-g) portions of the rested dough and roll each into a smooth, even ball. Place the balls on the prepared baking sheet, leaving space between them. Cover the balls with a damp tea towel and let them rest, watching as they grow even softer, ready to be transformed, another 30 minutes to 1 hour.

In a large heavy pot, heat the oil to 350°F (175°C). Gently lower the dough balls into the hot oil, frying three or four at a time, listening to the sizzle and watching them puff up and turn golden brown, 1 to 2 minutes per side. Flip them gently with chopsticks or tongs, ensuring each side gets its moment in the heat. Remove with a slotted spoon and place on a wire rack to cool.

MAKE THE WHISKEY PASTRY CREAM

In a medium saucepan, combine the milk, whiskey, and ¼ cup (50g) of the sugar and heat over medium heat until it just begins to steam, releasing a warm, inviting aroma. If using a vanilla bean, add it now, letting its flavor infuse the milk. Remove the pan from the heat.

In a medium bowl, whisk together the egg yolks, the remaining ¼ cup (50g) sugar, and the cornstarch until pale and silky.

Slowly whisk the warmed milk mixture into the egg yolk mixture to temper it, adding a little at a time until fully combined. Return the mixture to the saucepan and cook over medium heat, whisking continuously until it thickens into a luxurious cream. Let it bubble gently for 1 to 2 minutes, allowing the whiskey flavor to fully infuse the cream.

Remove the pan from the heat, discard the vanilla bean, if using, and whisk in the cubed butter and the vanilla extract, if using. Watch as the butter melts into the cream, creating a glossy, irresistible texture.

Pour the pastry cream into a clean bowl, pressing plastic wrap directly onto the surface to prevent a skin from forming. Let the pastry cream cool to room temperature, then transfer it to the refrigerator to chill completely. The cream should be thoroughly cold and set before using.

ASSEMBLE THE WHISKEY CRÈME BRÛLÉE BOMBS

Fill a piping bag fitted with a medium round tip with the chilled pastry cream. Poke a hole in the side of each cooled donut with a skewer and fill it generously with the cream, making sure it spills into every corner of the donut's soft, fluffy interior.

Pour the sugar for the topping into a shallow bowl and roll each filled donut in the sugar, coating it completely. Use a kitchen torch to caramelize the sugar on top, watching it melt and bubble into a golden, crackling layer. Repeat, adding more sugar and caramelizing again until you achieve a thick, glossy brûlée crust.

Top each donut with a candied orange slice for a bright, zesty finish. Serve while the brûlée is freshly torched and crackling, the whiskey cream cool and sinful. Every bite is pure seduction.

All right, you're in for a treat. These pleasure bombs are little pieces of heaven, and they're all about giving you that perfect, golden crunch followed by a soft, velvety filling. They're customizable too—whether you want to fill them with luscious pastry cream, gooey Nutella, or your favorite jam, every bite is an invitation to indulge. As I always say, these aren't just donuts; they're moments of pure, unrestrained pleasure. So, let's get to it—prepare yourself for a taste explosion that only Donut Daddy can deliver.

My Pleasure Bombs

MAKES 25 TO 30 DONUT BALLS

FOR THE DONUTS

4 cups (560g) bread flour

¼ cup (50g) granulated sugar

¾ teaspoon kosher salt

2 teaspoons active dry yeast

1 teaspoon dough improver (see page 20; optional)

1⅔ cups (395ml) filtered water (see page 20), at room temperature

¼ cup (55g) unsalted butter or vegetable shortening, cubed

Vegetable oil for frying (about 5 quarts [4.8L], depending on pot size)

FOR THE PASTRY CREAM

2 cups (475ml) whole milk

½ cup (100g) granulated sugar

1 vanilla bean, split and seeds scraped (optional, if not using vanilla extract)

4 egg yolks

¼ cup (35g) cornstarch

2 tablespoons unsalted butter, cubed

1 teaspoon pure vanilla extract (optional, if not using a vanilla bean)

One 16-ounce (450-g) jar Nutella or spread of choice for filling

One 16-ounce (450-g) jar jam of choice for filling

Confectioners' sugar for dusting

Superfine or caster sugar for dusting

MAKE THE DONUTS

In the bowl of a stand mixer fitted with the dough hook, combine the bread flour, granulated sugar, salt, yeast, and dough improver (if using).

With the mixer on low speed, slowly pour in the water, letting it blend in like a soft whisper. Add the cubed butter and mix until the dough begins to come together, 3 minutes.

Increase the mixer speed to medium and knead the dough, allowing it to transform into a smooth, elastic mass, 10 to 15 minutes. Keep the dough's temperature below 84°F (29°C) to maintain a perfect texture. Test it by stretching a small piece between your fingers, teasing it into a delicate windowpane (see page 20).

Grease a large bowl and transfer the dough to the bowl. Cover the bowl with plastic wrap and let the dough rest in a warm, dry place, giving it time to double in size, like it's getting ready for its big debut, 1 hour.

CONTINUED

My Pleasure Bombs

Lightly flour a baking sheet. Weigh out portions of rested dough of about 1¼ ounces (35g) each, rolling them into smooth balls. They should feel light and tender in your hands, ready to become golden miracles. Place the dough balls on the prepared baking sheet, leaving space between them. Cover the balls with a damp tea towel and let them rest for another 30 minutes to 1 hour. This will make them softer, fluffier, and even more irresistible.

In a large heavy pot, heat the oil to 350°F (175°C). Gently lower the dough balls into the hot oil, frying three or four at a time, watching as they puff up and turn a beautiful golden brown, 1 to 2 minutes per side. Flip them gently with chopsticks or tongs, savoring each moment as they take on their final form. Remove with a slotted spoon and place on a wire rack to cool slightly.

MAKE THE PASTRY CREAM

In a medium saucepan, combine the milk and ¼ cup (50g) of the sugar and heat over medium heat until the mixture just begins to steam. If using a vanilla bean, add it now to infuse the milk with its sweet, warm aroma. Remove from the heat and let the mixture steep for a few minutes.

In a medium bowl, whisk together the egg yolks, the remaining ¼ cup (50g) sugar, and the cornstarch until pale and smooth.

Slowly pour the hot milk mixture into the egg yolk mixture, adding a little at a time and whisking continuously to temper the eggs and prevent curdling. Return the mixture to the saucepan and cook over medium heat, whisking continuously, until it thickens into a luscious, velvety cream. Let it bubble gently for 1 to 2 minutes, to cook out the cornstarch.

Remove from the heat, discard the vanilla bean, if using, and whisk in the cubed butter and the vanilla extract, if using. The cream should be rich, smooth, and irresistibly glossy.

Pour the pastry cream into a clean bowl. Cover the cream with plastic wrap, pressing it directly onto the surface to prevent a skin from forming. Let it cool to room temperature, then refrigerate until completely chilled. The cream should be thoroughly cold and set before using.

ASSEMBLE THE PLEASURE BOMBS

Fill three individual piping bags fitted with a small round tip with the Nutella, jam, and cold pastry cream, respectively, creating a variety of indulgent fillings.

Once the donuts have cooled, dust them generously with confectioners' sugar for that extra touch of sweetness, making them look like little snowy pillows of delight.

Use the piping bags to fill each donut to the brim with your desired filling, letting the donut give way to the creamy, rich interior as you fill it.

For a final touch, dust the donuts lightly with superfine sugar, stacking them upright so that each filling peeks out, giving everyone a glimpse of the decadent surprises inside. Serve these delightful donut bombs fresh, with gooey centers ready to delight with every bite.

Don't worry, my sweet—Donut Daddy doesn't do bland, chalky, pretend desserts that promise you the world. These are the real deal: rich cocoa, velvety protein icing, and just enough sweetness to keep you on your toes. You'll feel like you're cheating, but your macros will thank me. These donuts aren't just a snack, they're a statement. Perfect for a postworkout treat or a breakfast that says, "Yeah, I've got this." Each bite is proof that with Donut Daddy, you really can have it all. For an extra boost of nutrition, you can use oat flour in place of all-purpose, bringing a gluten-free, fiber-rich twist to these protein-packed donuts. I also use egg replacer to keep things accessible for vegans and anyone with an egg allergy. Donut Daddy's got you!

Protein Donuts

MAKES 8 TO 10 DONUTS

FOR THE DONUTS

¾ cup (105g) all-purpose flour

⅓ cup (50g) protein powder of choice (I recommend vanilla whey)

1 teaspoon baking powder

½ teaspoon baking soda

1 teaspoon egg replacer (such as Bob's Red Mill) or 1 real egg

3 tablespoons unsweetened Dutch-processed cocoa powder

2 tablespoons honey or maple syrup, preferably Grade B

1½ tablespoons coconut oil

½ cup (120g) applesauce

¾ cup (180g) coconut yogurt

FOR THE PROTEIN ICING

½ cup (160g) maple syrup, preferably grade B (use half sugar-free for lower sugar)

½ cup (80g) protein powder

2 tablespoons smooth peanut butter or nut butter of choice

Crushed peanuts for garnish

MAKE THE DONUTS

Preheat the oven to 350°F (175°C). Lightly spray two donut pans with nonstick spray to prevent sticking.

In the bowl of a stand mixer fitted with the paddle attachment, combine the flour, protein powder, baking powder, baking soda, egg replacer, and cocoa powder and mix on low speed for 2 minutes to ensure even distribution.

In a separate bowl, whisk together the honey, coconut oil, applesauce, and coconut yogurt until smooth and slightly glossy.

Gradually add the yogurt mixture to the flour mixture and mix to combine. Increase the mixer speed to medium and blend for 3 minutes. The batter should be thick yet pourable, like a silky chocolate dream.

CONTINUED

Protein Donuts

Fill a piping bag fitted with a large round tip with the batter. Pipe the batter into the prepared donut pans filling each shape about three-quarters full to leave room for the donuts to rise.

Bake the donuts until they feel springy to the touch and smell like pure cocoa heaven, 15 minutes. Let them cool in the pans for 5 minutes before transferring them to a wire rack.

MAKE THE PROTEIN ICING

In a small saucepan, combine the maple syrup, protein powder, and peanut butter and heat over low heat, stirring continuously, until the mixture reaches 176°F (80°C). The icing should be smooth, thick, and shiny, like liquid gold.

ASSEMBLE THE PROTEIN DONUTS

While the donuts are still slightly warm, dip the tops into the protein icing, letting the glaze coat them in a rich, glossy layer. Feel free to let the icing drip down the sides for added drama.

Garnish with crushed nuts. The crunch and sweetness will take these donuts to the next level.

Allow the icing to set for a few minutes (if you have the patience) before serving.

You think you've had chocolate donuts before, huh? Sweetheart, you've never had anything like these. These donuts are a full-on experience. Imagine biting into rich, cocoa-kissed cake, a silky peanut butter center, and a glossy salted caramel glaze dripping with temptation. And, of course, there's a cheeky little peanut butter cup perched on top, daring you to indulge. Go ahead, take a bite! I'll wait patiently . . .

Sinful Chocolate Seduction Donuts

MAKES 10 TO 15 DONUTS

FOR THE DONUTS

3 cups (420g) bread flour

½ cup (40g) unsweetened Dutch-processed cocoa powder

¼ cup (50g) granulated sugar

¾ teaspoon kosher salt

2 teaspoons active dry yeast

1 teaspoon dough improver (see page 20; optional)

1⅔ cups (395ml) filtered water (see page 20), at room temperature

¼ cup (55g) unsalted butter, cubed

Vegetable oil for frying (about 5 quarts [4.8L], depending on pot size)

FOR THE PEANUT BUTTER CENTER

2 cups (240g) unsalted roasted peanuts

¼ teaspoon kosher salt

1 ounce dark chocolate, melted

FOR THE SALTED CARAMEL GLAZE

½ cup (110g) unsalted butter

¾ cup (150g) packed light brown sugar

½ cup (120ml) heavy cream

1 teaspoon kosher salt

¾ cup (135g) blond chocolate disks (I recommend Valrhona Dulcey or Callebaut Gold)

1½ cups (180g) confectioners' sugar

10 to 15 mini peanut butter cups (one for each donut), chopped for topping

MAKE THE DONUTS

In the bowl of a stand mixer fitted with the dough hook, combine the bread flour, cocoa powder, granulated sugar, salt, yeast, and dough improver (if using).

With the mixer on low speed, slowly pour in the water, letting it blend in. Add the cubed butter and mix until the dough begins to form, 2 to 3 minutes.

Increase the mixer speed to medium and knead the dough until it is smooth, elastic, and slightly tacky, 10 to 15 minutes. Keep the dough's temperature below 84°F (29°C) to maintain a perfect texture. Test it by stretching a small piece between your fingers, teasing it into a delicate windowpane (see page 20).

CONTINUED

Sinful Chocolate Seduction Donuts

CONTINUED

Grease a large bowl and transfer the dough to the bowl. Cover the bowl with plastic wrap and let the dough rise in a warm, dry place until doubled in size, 1 hour.

Lightly flour a baking sheet. Divide the rested dough into 2½-ounce (75-g) portions, rolling each into a smooth ball. Place the dough balls on the prepared baking sheet, leaving space between them. Cover the balls with a damp tea towel and let them rest for 45 minutes (the dough needs extra time to proof because cocoa powder slows down the yeast).

In a large heavy pot, heat the oil to 350°F (175°C). Gently lower the dough balls into the hot oil, frying two or three at a time, until they are puffed and golden brown, 1 to 2 minutes per side. Flip them gently with chopsticks or tongs, savoring each moment as they take on their final form. Remove with a slotted spoon and place on a wire rack to cool completely.

MAKE THE PEANUT BUTTER CENTER

In a food processor, grind the peanuts until smooth and creamy, 10 to 15 minutes. Add the salt and melted chocolate, blending until fully incorporated, another 1 to 2 minutes. Let the peanut butter cool to room temperature.

MAKE THE SALTED CARAMEL GLAZE

In a saucepan, combine the butter and brown sugar and melt over medium heat, stirring until the sugar dissolves. Stir in the cream and salt and simmer until slightly thickened, 3 to 4 minutes.

Remove from the heat and stir in the blond chocolate until melted and smooth. Gradually add the confectioners' sugar, whisking until the glaze is glossy and slightly thickened. If the glaze is too thin, let it cool slightly to thicken.

ASSEMBLE THE SINFUL CHOCOLATE SEDUCTION DONUTS

Fill a piping bag fitted with a small round tip with the peanut butter center. Poke a hole in the side of each donut with a skewer and pipe the peanut butter center into the hole. You'll feel the donut plump up as the creamy filling spills into every corner.

Dip the filled donuts into the salted caramel glaze, coating the tops completely. Crown each donut with some of the mini peanut butter cup pieces, pressing them gently into the glaze for a picture-perfect finish.

Serve these indulgent treats fresh and slightly warm, with the salted caramel glaze still glossy and the peanut butter center perfectly creamy.

"Apple pie donuts?" you ask, tilting your head. "Sounds basic." I chuckle, leaning closer, my voice dropping to a playful whisper. "Oh, darling, these are not your ordinary treats. These are my Cinnamon Apple Bombshells: crispy on the outside, soft on the inside, and oozing with warm apple pie filling. Basic? Not with Donut Daddy. Let me show you how it's done." Note: For the cookie crumbs, feel free to replace with your favorite store-bought version.

Cinnamon Apple Bombshells

MAKES 12 TO 15 DONUTS

FOR THE DONUTS

4 cups (560g) bread flour

¼ cup (50g) granulated sugar

¾ teaspoon kosher salt

2 teaspoons active dry yeast

1 teaspoon dough improver (see page 20; optional)

1⅔ cups (395ml) filtered water (see page 20), at room temperature

¼ cup (55g) unsalted butter or vegetable shortening, cubed

Vegetable oil for frying (about 5 quarts [4.8L], depending on pot size)

FOR THE COOKIE CRUMBS

½ cup (110g) unsalted butter, softened

½ cup (100g) granulated sugar

½ teaspoon pure vanilla extract

1 egg, at room temperature

2 cups (280g) all-purpose flour

2 tablespoons cornstarch

1 teaspoon baking powder

1 tablespoon whole milk

FOR THE APPLE PIE FILLING

¼ cup (55g) unsalted butter

2 teaspoons ground cinnamon

8 medium apples (such as Gala or Lady Alice), peeled, cored, and chopped

⅔ cup (130g) granulated sugar

6 tablespoons (90ml) filtered water (see page 20)

2 tablespoons cornstarch

¼ cup (60ml) tap water

FOR THE VANILLA GLAZE

4¾ cups (570g) confectioners' sugar

Seeds from 1 vanilla bean

½ cup (120ml) hot tap water

MAKE THE DONUTS

In the bowl of a stand mixer fitted with the dough hook, combine the bread flour, granulated sugar, salt, yeast, and dough improver (if using). Give it a quick mix.

With the mixer on low speed, slowly pour in the filtered water. Add the cubed butter, letting it incorporate into the mixture. Mix until the dough starts to come together, 3 minutes.

Increase the mixer speed to medium and knead the dough until it becomes soft, elastic, and slightly tacky, 10 to 15 minutes. The dough should feel like a smooth, pliable dream beneath your touch.

CONTINUED

Cinnamon Apple Bombshells

CONTINUED

Grease a large bowl and transfer the dough to the bowl. Cover the bowl with plastic wrap and let the dough rise in a warm, dry place, doubling in size, 1 hour.

Lightly flour a baking sheet. Divide the rested dough into 2½-ounce (75-g) balls, rolling each one with care. Place them on the prepared baking sheet, leaving space between them. Cover the balls with a damp tea towel and let them rest until puffed and pillowy, another 30 minutes.

In a large heavy pot, heat the oil to 350°F (175°C). Gently lower the dough balls one at a time into the hot oil, watching them sizzle and puff up like golden treasures. Fry two or three dough balls at a time, ensuring they have enough space to float and cook evenly, 1 to 2 minutes on each side. Flip them gently with chopsticks or tongs. Remove with a slotted spoon and place on a wire rack to cool slightly.

MAKE THE COOKIE CRUMBS (SKIP THIS STEP IF YOU WANT TO USE YOUR FAVORITE STORE-BOUGHT COOKIE.)

Preheat the oven to 350°F (175°C).

In the bowl of a stand mixer fitted with the paddle attachment, combine the softened butter, granulated sugar, and vanilla and beat on medium speed until light and fluffy, 3 minutes. Add the egg and mix until fully incorporated, another 2 minutes.

Sift together the all-purpose flour, cornstarch, and baking powder. Add the flour mixture to the batter, along with the milk. Lower the mixer speed to low and mix until a soft dough forms, 1 to 2 minutes.

Line a baking sheet with parchment paper. Scoop the dough into tablespoon-size balls with an ice-cream scoop. Flatten the balls into disks and place them, evenly spaced, on the prepared baking sheet.

Bake until golden, 15 minutes. Place on a wire rack to cool completely.

Using a resealable bag, place the cookies in the bag and crush them with a rolling pin into rough, pea-size crumbs.

MAKE THE APPLE PIE FILLING

In a large saucepan, melt the butter over medium heat. Add the cinnamon and stir until fragrant. Toss in the chopped apples, granulated sugar, and filtered water. Cover and cook, stirring occasionally, until slightly softened, 4 to 6 minutes.

In a small dish, combine the cornstarch and tap water and mix to make a slurry. Stir the slurry into the apple mixture and cook, stirring continuously, until the filling thickens and the apples are softer but not mushy, 2 to 3 minutes. Remove from the heat and let the filling cool to room temperature.

MAKE THE VANILLA GLAZE

In a large bowl, combine the confectioners' sugar and vanilla bean seeds and stir together. Gradually add the hot tap water, stirring until the glaze is smooth and glossy.

ASSEMBLE THE CINNAMON APPLE BOMBSHELLS

Fill a piping bag fitted with a #12 tip (½ inch [13 mm] circular tip) with the cooled apple pie filling. Pierce the side of each donut with a skewer and pipe generously to fill the hole until the filling bursts out just slightly.

Dip the tops of the filled donuts into the vanilla glaze, letting the glossy coating wrap around each donut like a loving caress.

Pour the cookie crumbs into a shallow bowl and roll the glazed donuts in the crumbs, ensuring every surface is coated in that buttery, crumbly goodness. Let the donuts sit for 10 minutes to firm up the glaze. If you have any extra filling left, pipe it on top of the bombshells for an extra-decadent hit.

Serve these golden delights with their cookie-coated shells and their gooey apple centers. One bite and you'll understand why Donut Daddy's creations leave everyone asking for more.

Darling, do you feel that? The tension in the air? It's chocolate calling, begging for attention. Tonight, I'll let you in on a secret that's left lovers swooning and rivals speechless: Chocolate Bliss Bombs. Bite into one and you'll understand why they're banned in three countries for being too . . . pleasurable.

You'll get your hands dirty, you'll sweat, but oh, when you experience that first taste? You'll thank the Donut Daddy for delivering the ultimate treat. Let's get messy.

Donut Daddy's Chocolate Bliss Bombs

MAKES 12 REGULAR DONUTS OR 24 INDULGENT DONUT HOLES

FOR THE DONUTS

½ cup (120ml) whole milk, warmed

¼ cup (60ml) warm filtered water (see page 20)

2¼ teaspoons (1 packet) active dry yeast

2½ cups (350g) all-purpose flour

¼ cup (50g) granulated sugar

1 tablespoon baking powder

½ teaspoon ground cinnamon

¼ teaspoon kosher salt

1 egg

2 tablespoons unsalted butter, melted

½ teaspoon pure vanilla extract

Vegetable oil for frying (about 5 quarts [4.8L], depending on pot size)

FOR THE CHOCOLATE GLAZE

¾ cup (90g) confectioners' sugar

2 tablespoons unsweetened Dutch-processed cocoa powder

2 tablespoons whole milk

1 teaspoon pure vanilla extract

FOR THE BUTTERNUT COATING

1¼ cups (100g) finely shredded unsweetened coconut flakes

½ cup (100g) granulated sugar

1 teaspoon orange food coloring

MAKE THE DONUTS

Start by whispering sweet nothings to your yeast. In a bowl, combine the war m milk and water (the mixture should be at 110°F [43°C]). Sprinkle the yeast on top and let it froth like it's falling in love, 5 to 10 minutes.

In the bowl of a stand mixer fitted with the paddle attachment, combine the flour, granulated sugar, baking powder, cinnamon, and salt and mix on low speed until it's just a tease of a mixture, 1 minute.

CONTINUED

Donut Daddy's Chocolate Bliss Bombs

CONTINUED

Swap in the dough hook. Add the frothy yeast mixture, the egg, melted butter, and vanilla. With the mixer on medium speed, knead the mixture until the dough is soft, supple, and begging for attention, 5 minutes.

Grease a large bowl and gently place the dough in the bowl. Cover the bowl with a damp tea towel, like a cozy little blanket, and let the dough rise in a warm, dry place for 1 to 1½ hours. It should double in size. Don't we all with the right touch?

On a lightly floured surface, roll out the rested dough to a ½-inch (1.3-cm) thickness. Use a 3-inch (7.5-cm) donut cutter for rings or a smaller 1-inch (2.5-cm) round cutter for donut-hole-size bliss bombs.

Lightly flour a baking sheet. Lay the donuts out on the prepared baking sheet, leaving space between them. Let them rest for 15 minutes. Things are about to heat up.

In a large heavy pot, heat the oil to 350°F (175°C). Gently lower the dough rings in batches of three or four into the hot oil, watching them sizzle and puff up like golden treasures, 1 to 2 minutes on each side. Flip them gently with chopsticks or tongs. Remove with a slotted spoon and place on a wire rack to cool slightly.

MAKE THE CHOCOLATE GLAZE

In a medium mixing bowl, whisk together the confectioners' sugar, cocoa powder, milk, and vanilla until smooth, shiny, and ready to drizzle seduction onto your donuts.

MAKE THE BUTTERNUT COATING

In a separate mixing bowl, combine the coconut, granulated sugar, and food coloring and stir until it's vibrant and ready to embrace that chocolaty glaze.

ASSEMBLE THE DONUT DADDY'S CHOCOLATE BLISS BOMBS

Dip each donut into the chocolate glaze, let the glaze drip off provocatively, then roll the donut in the butternut coating. Press gently to make sure the coating sticks—no half measures here. Let the donuts sit for 5 minutes.

Serve with a wink and a knowing smile. Don't forget to warn your guests: One mouthful and they'll be chasing the Donut Daddy for more.

Close your eyes and picture this: golden, thick churros that beg to be dipped, dusted, and devoured. They're longer, stronger, and tastier than any you've ever had before. Baby, this isn't just dessert, it's a love affair. Grab your piping bag and let me take you on a churro journey you'll never forget.

Churro Obsessions

MAKES 12 TO 16 EXTRA-THICK CHURROS, EACH 6 TO 8 INCHES (15 TO 20CM) LONG

FOR THE CHURROS

2 cups (480ml) filtered water (see page 20)

½ teaspoon kosher salt

2 teaspoons pure vanilla extract

½ cup (110g) unsalted butter

2 tablespoons sugar

4 cups (560g) all-purpose flour

4 eggs

Vegetable oil for frying (about 5 quarts [4.8L], depending on pot size)

FOR THE CINNAMON SUGAR COATING

1 cup (200g) sugar

2 teaspoons ground cinnamon

Melted chocolate for serving

Creamy caramel sauce, homemade (see page 211) or store-bought, for serving

Dulce de leche, store-bought, for serving

MAKE THE CHURROS

In a medium saucepan, combine the water, salt, vanilla, butter, and sugar and bring to a gentle boil over medium heat, stirring occasionally.

Lower the heat to low and stir in the flour all at once. Keep mixing until a soft, shiny dough forms, pulling away from the sides of the pan. It's giving glossy perfection, just like you deserve.

Into the bowl of a stand mixer fitted with a paddle attachment, transfer the dough and let it cool slightly. With mixer on medium speed, gradually add the eggs, one at a time, until the dough is smooth, luscious, and pipe ready.

Scoop the dough into a piping bag fitted with a 16mm star tip. Make sure it's ready to go, because it's got a big job ahead. Also, line a wire rack with paper towels and set aside.

In a large heavy pot, heat the oil to a sizzling 350°F (175°C). Working confidently, pipe 3 to 4 strips of dough 6 to 8 inches (15 to 20cm) long directly into the hot oil. Use scissors to cut the dough cleanly as it slides into its golden bath. Fry until your churros are beautifully golden and slightly puffed, 2 to 3 minutes per side. Flip with chopsticks or tongs. Remove with a slotted spoon and place on the prepared wire rack to drain away the excess oil (but keep them tantalizingly crispy).

Churro Obsessions

MAKE THE CINNAMON SUGAR COATING

In a shallow bowl, stir together the sugar and cinnamon until fully incorporated.

ASSEMBLE THE CHURRO OBSESSIONS

While the churros are still warm (and ready to mingle), toss them generously in the cinnamon sugar. Let each one get a perfect, shimmering coat because they do deserve it.

Serve these beauties with dipping sauces like velvety chocolate, creamy caramel, or dulce de leche for a drizzle of pure decadence. Don't wait too long to enjoy these churros. Life's too short for cold desserts.

O2

Mix and Chill

A Lover's Guide to Quick and Irresistible Desserts

Welcome to the part of the book where things get steamy, creamy, and downright dreamy. You've entered my dessert boudoir, the sacred space where chocolate flows, dough rises (if you know what I mean), and every chew whispers sweet nothings to your taste buds. You didn't come here to behave, did you? Good, because neither did I.

Here in the Donut Daddy's den, it's all about dim lights, soft sighs, and the kind of recipes that could make even the most stoic saint break into a sweat. These desserts are the reason the "Are you still watching?" message pops up on Netflix. One bite and you won't just chill, you'll go straight down into a thrill, and I mean faster than my Matcha Me, Honey panna cotta on a hot summer night.

If you're familiar with how I do things, you already know I don't just bake; I make love to my desserts. I slap that dough with the enthusiasm of someone who's had just enough espresso, tease my fillings until they're perfectly piped, and drizzle chocolate so slowly and sensually it could probably be flagged. And when I torch a meringue, I swear the flames get envious of the heat I bring.

So, my sweet little rebels, are you ready to bake your way into ecstasy? Then let's roll.

Ever had a dessert whisper in your ear and tell you you're its favorite? This one does. And the flames . . . Just a little heat to match the passion you'll feel after the first bite. These crepes are thin, delicate, and unapologetically drenched in citrusy caramel sauce and flambéed for maximum drama. Let's light this fire together, shall we?

Crepes Tease Suzette

MAKES 10 CREPES, 6 TO 8 SERVINGS

FOR THE CREPES

2 eggs

¾ cup (105g) all-purpose flour

½ cup (120ml) whole milk

½ teaspoon sugar

⅛ teaspoon kosher salt

⅓ cup (80ml) cold filtered water (see page 20)

1 tablespoon canola oil

1 tablespoon unsalted butter, melted

FOR THE ORANGE BUTTER SAUCE

½ cup (110g) unsalted butter, softened

⅓ cup (65g) sugar

1½ teaspoons finely grated orange zest (from about 1 orange)

⅓ cup (80ml) freshly squeezed orange juice (from about 2 medium oranges)

2 tablespoons sugar to finish

3 tablespoons orange liqueur (such as Grand Marnier or Cointreau) for flambéing

1 tablespoon Cognac for flambéing

1 to 2 extra tablespoons freshly squeezed orange juice, plus a few orange segments (fresh or from a jar) for finishing (optional)

MAKE THE CREPES (MANUALLY OR MIXER)

In a medium bowl, whisk together the eggs, flour, milk, sugar, and salt until smooth. If you want to keep it hands-on (like Daddy prefers), grab your trusty hand whisk and go to town until the batter feels smooth, pourable, and thick enough to coat the back of a spoon, but not clingy.

If you're in a rush and craving precision, use a stand mixer with the whisk attachment on low speed until everything is well combined, about 1 minute.

Slowly add the water, oil, and melted butter, whisking until the batter flows like a smooth operator. Let the batter rest for 15 minutes.

Have a baking sheet nearby. Set a 10-inch (25-cm) crepe pan or nonstick skillet over medium-high heat. Brush it lightly with butter. Don't be shy; your pan loves the attention. Pour in 3 tablespoons of the batter, tilting the pan in a circular motion, like you're seducing the batter to spread evenly.

Cook until the edges curl up slightly and golden spots appear, about 45 seconds. Slide a long spatula underneath and give the crepe a confident flip. Cook until just kissed with color, another 10 to 15 seconds. Transfer to the nearby baking sheet and repeat. You should get about 10 crepes.

CONTINUED

Crepes Tease Suzette

CONTINUED

MAKE THE ORANGE BUTTER SAUCE

In a food processor, combine the softened butter, sugar, and the orange zest and blend until smooth. While blending, slowly pour in the orange juice. The mixture should come together like a silky, citrusy daydream.

Transfer the mixture to a large flame-proof skillet over medium heat. Stir occasionally as the mixture bubbles and thickens into a glossy, syrupy sauce, about 5 minutes.

ASSEMBLE THE CREPES TEASE SUZETTE

Lower the heat to low. Working one at a time, take a crepe and gently dip both sides in the sauce, letting it soak up the magic. Fold the crepe into quarters, showing off its best side (crepes love to pose). Let any extra sauce drip back into the skillet, then place the crepe on a baking sheet or plate. Repeat for all the crepes.

If you'd like your sauce thinner or more citrus-forward (as shown in the photo), stir in 1 to 2 tablespoons of additional freshly squeezed orange juice and a few orange segments into the skillet after all the crepes have been folded and set aside. Simmer briefly on low heat to warm through.

THE GRAND FINALE (FLAMBÉ!)

Return the folded crepes to the skillet, layering them gently to fully cover the bottom of the pan. Sprinkle with 2 tablespoons sugar.

Place the skillet over medium heat and add the orange liqueur and Cognac. Using a long-handled lighter, carefully ignite the sauce. Spoon the flaming sauce over the crepes. Let the flames subside before portioning the crepes to individual plates.

Serve the crepes and spoon extra sauce from the skillet over each plate.

What is better than a tartlet that melts in your mouth and leaves you weak in the knees? Nothing. We're talking a velvety cocoa sablée crust cradling caramelized bananas, crowned with clouds of Chantilly cream and finished with a brûléed banana that crackles under your spoon. Unlike the soft, pillowy doughs we've explored so far, this recipe features pâte sablée, a classic French pastry known for its delicate, buttery crumb. Unlike donut dough, which relies on yeast or baking powder for lightness, sablée dough is a short-crust pastry, meaning there's minimal rise but maximum richness. And did I mention it has a melt-in-your-mouth texture?

Cream Me Up Tartlets

MAKES 8 TARTLETS

FOR THE COCOA SABLÉE DOUGH

2 cups (280g) all-purpose flour

3 tablespoons unsweetened Dutch-processed cocoa powder

¼ teaspoon baking powder

Pinch of kosher salt

½ cup (100g) granulated sugar

½ cup plus 1½ teaspoons (120g) cold unsalted butter, cubed

1 egg

FOR THE CARAMELIZED BANANAS

3½ tablespoons unsalted butter

⅓ cup (65g) packed light brown sugar

3 ripe bananas, sliced into wheels

1 teaspoon pure vanilla extract

Pinch of ground cinnamon (optional)

1 cup (240ml) Chantilly Cream (page 206)

1 ripe banana, sliced into 8 rounds, for garnish

1½ tablespoons superfine or caster sugar for garnish

MAKE THE COCOA SABLÉE DOUGH

Into the bowl of a stand mixer fitted with the paddle attachment, sift the flour, cocoa powder, baking powder, and salt. With the mixer on low speed, stir in the granulated sugar. Add the cold butter and mix until the mixture resembles coarse crumbs. (If you're feeling hands-on, use your fingertips to rub the butter in.)

With the mixer still on low, add the egg and mix until the dough just comes together. Turn the dough out onto a lightly floured surface and gently press it into a smooth, uniform disk—avoid overworking it to keep the delicate texture. Wrap the dough tightly in plastic wrap to prevent drying out, then place it directly in the refrigerator (no bowl needed). Let it chill for 1 hour until firm but pliable. If the dough feels too stiff after chilling, let it rest at room temperature for 5 to 10 minutes before rolling it out.

CONTINUED

Cream Me Up Tartlets

Preheat the oven to 350°F (175°C). Gather eight 4-inch (10-cm) tartlet rings. Line a baking sheet with parchment paper and set aside—this will hold the tartlets during baking.

Place the dough between two silicone mats or pieces of parchment paper and roll the dough to ⅛ inch (3mm) thick. If it gets too soft, pop it in the fridge for a few minutes to firm up.

Using your tartlet rings as a guide, cut the rolled dough into circles slightly larger than your tartlet rings. Grease the rings and press the dough into them, ensuring the edges are even and smooth.

Place the tartlets on the reserved baking sheet. Layer a piece of parchment paper and baking weights (or dried beans) on top of the dough to prevent puffing. Bake until the edges look set and dry, 13 minutes. Cool completely in the rings on the baking sheet before unmolding the tartlets from the rings.

MAKE THE CARAMELIZED BANANAS

In a medium saucepan, melt the butter over medium heat until foamy. Add the brown sugar and stir until the mixture forms a smooth caramel, 2 to 3 minutes. Add the banana wheels, cooking them until golden and soft but not mushy, 2 to 3 minutes per side. Stir in the vanilla and cinnamon (if using). Let the caramelized bananas cool slightly before filling the tartlets.

ASSEMBLE THE TARTLETS

Fill a piping bag fitted with a ¼- to 5⁄16-inch (6- to 8-mm) round tip with the Chantilly cream.

Spoon the caramelized bananas into each chocolate tartlet base, smoothing the top with a small metal spatula. Pipe the Chantilly cream onto the tartlets in elegant, peaked shapes.

For the garnish, lay the banana rounds on a heatproof surface or a parchment-lined baking sheet. Sprinkle superfine sugar evenly on top of each round. Brûlée the rounds with a kitchen torch until golden and crackly, moving the flame in small circles to caramelize evenly without burning. Let them cool slightly, then place one round in the center of each tartlet as the pièce de résistance.

Cannolis and Chill is here to satisfy your dessert cravings with crispy, golden tubes of fried dough and a chocolate-studded mascarpone filling that's smooth as silk. Sweet Marsala? Oh yes. Mascarpone? Obviously. This is the kind of dessert that leans in close and says, "Just one more bite," until you're shamelessly licking the bowl.

Cannolis and Chill

MAKES 8 SERVINGS

FOR THE SHELLS

3 cups (420g) all-purpose flour

¼ cup (50g) granulated sugar

¼ teaspoon ground cinnamon

3 tablespoons vegetable shortening

½ cup (120ml) sweet Marsala wine

2 tablespoons filtered water (see page 20)

1 tablespoon distilled white vinegar

1 egg plus 1 egg yolk

Vegetable oil for frying (about 1 quart [950ml], depending on pot size)

FOR THE CANNOLI FILLING

1¾ cups (415g) heavy cream

2 cups (480g) ricotta cheese, well drained

1 cup (240g) mascarpone cheese

2 teaspoons pure vanilla extract

¼ cup plus 2 tablespoons (75g) granulated sugar

½ cup (90g) mini semisweet chocolate chips

Crushed roasted pistachios for garnish

Confectioners' sugar for garnish

MAKE THE SHELLS

In the bowl of a stand mixer fitted with the paddle attachment, whisk together the flour, granulated sugar, and cinnamon. With the mixer on low speed, add the shortening and mix until the mixture resembles coarse crumbs. Slowly add the Marsala, water, vinegar, whole egg, and egg yolk and continue to mix until combined.

Switch to the dough hook and knead the dough on medium speed until the dough is smooth and elastic, 6 to 8 minutes. It should pass the windowpane test (see page 20). (If kneading by hand, work the dough until elastic, 10 to 12 minutes.) Wrap the dough in plastic wrap and let it rest at room temperature for 30 minutes.

On a lightly floured surface, roll the rested dough to about ⅟₁₆ inch (2mm) thick. Use a round cutter to cut circles about 4 inches (10 cm) in diameter. Wrap each circle around a metal cannoli tube, sealing the edge with a dab of egg wash.

In a large heavy pot, heat the oil to 350°F (175°C). Gently lower the wrapped tubes into the hot oil, frying three or four at a time. Fry until golden and crisp, 1 to 2 minutes, turning as needed for even browning. Remove with a slotted spoon and slide the shells off the molds once cool enough to handle. Drain on paper towels.

CONTINUED

Cannolis and Chill

MAKE THE CANNOLI FILLING

Chill the mixer bowl and whisk attachment of a stand mixer for 10 to 15 minutes.

In the chilled bowl of the stand mixer fitted with the chilled whisk attachment, whip the cream on medium speed until soft peaks form, 2 to 3 minutes. The cream should hold its shape but remain slightly pliable for easy folding. Set aside.

In a food processor, combine the ricotta, mascarpone, vanilla, and granulated sugar and process until smooth and creamy.

Transfer the mixture to a large mixing bowl to allow room for folding. Using a spatula, gently fold the whipped cream into the ricotta mixture, using light strokes to keep the filling light and airy. Stir in the mini chocolate chips as the final, irresistible touch. The cannoli filling should be thick, creamy, and stable enough to hold its shape in the shells. (This can be made ahead of time and stored in the refrigerator for up to 2 days.)

ASSEMBLE THE CANNOLIS AND CHILL

Spoon the creamy cannoli filling into a piping bag fitted with a round tip of choice. Stuff the golden cannoli shells with the filling until the filling is just peeking out of both sides of the shell. Sprinkle the creamy ends with crushed pistachios and scatter confectioners' sugar on top of the middle of the shell. These are tubular temptations just waiting to be devoured.

Pizza? For dessert? Don't act so shocked. This cocoa dessert pizza awakens all the senses, starting with a rich cocoa dough stuffed with Nutella and finishing with a decadent layer of hazelnut praline, fresh fruit, and creamy Chantilly swirls. You'll never look at pizza delivery the same way again.

Naughty Hazelnut Cocoa Pizza

MAKES ONE 12-INCH (30-CM) DESSERT PIZZA, 6 TO 8 SERVINGS

FOR THE HAZELNUT PRALINE PASTE

1½ cups (180g) hazelnuts

½ cup (100g) sugar

2 tablespoons tap water

Pinch of kosher salt

FOR THE WHITE CHOCOLATE CHANTILLY CREAM

7 ounces (200g) white chocolate, finely chopped

1¼ cups (300ml) heavy cream

1 teaspoon pure vanilla extract

FOR THE MILK CHOCOLATE CHANTILLY CREAM

7 ounces (200g) milk chocolate, finely chopped

1¼ cups (300ml) heavy cream

1 teaspoon pure vanilla extract

FOR THE COCOA DOUGH

3¾ cups (525g) all-purpose flour

3 tablespoons unsweetened Dutch-processed cocoa powder

¾ teaspoon active dry yeast

Pinch of kosher salt

1½ cups plus 2 tablespoons (390g) filtered water (see page 20), at room temperature

½ cup (150g) Nutella

¼ cup (40g) finely chopped dark or milk chocolate

½ cup (60g) fresh raspberries

½ cup (70g) quartered fresh strawberries

½ cup (70g) fresh blueberries

¼ cup (30g) fresh blackberries

½ cup (70g) chopped roasted hazelnuts

MAKE THE HAZELNUT PRALINE PASTE

Preheat the oven to 350°F (175°C).

Spread the hazelnuts on a baking sheet and roast for 10 minutes. Let them cool slightly, then rub off the skins using a towel, leaving the peeled hazelnuts on the baking sheet.

In a medium saucepan, combine the sugar and tap water and heat over medium heat, stirring gently until the sugar dissolves. Bring the mixture to a simmer, then lower the heat slightly and continue to cook without stirring until the caramel turns a golden amber color, 8 to 10 minutes. If needed, swirl the pan occasionally to ensure even caramelization. Once the caramel is golden brown, immediately pour it over the prepared hazelnuts on the baking sheet. Let the caramelized hazelnuts cool completely until hardened.

Break the caramelized hazelnuts into smaller pieces and transfer them to a food processor. Add the salt and blend for several minutes until smooth, scraping down the sides of the bowl as needed.

CONTINUED

Naughty Hazelnut Cocoa Pizza

CONTINUED

MAKE THE WHITE AND MILK CHOCOLATE CHANTILLY CREAMS

In a microwavable bowl, melt the white chocolate on medium (50%) power in 30-second intervals, stirring after each interval, until fully melted, 1 to 2 minutes total.

In a small saucepan, heat ⅓ cup (100ml) of the cream over medium-low heat until it is hot but not boiling (about 175°F/80°C). The cream should be steaming and just beginning to form small bubbles around the edges but not come to a full simmer. Stir the warmed cream into the melted chocolate. Cool the mixture to room temperature, then chill in the refrigerator for 2 hours.

In the bowl of a stand mixer fitted with the whisk attachment, combine the chilled chocolate mixture, the remaining cream (0.85 cup/200ml), and the vanilla, and whip on medium-high speed until soft peaks form, 2 to 3 minutes. Store in an airtight container in the refrigerator for up to 2 days. Repeat with the same steps but with milk chocolate for the Milk Chocolate Chantilly Cream.

MAKE THE COCOA DOUGH

In a stand mixer fitted with a dough hook, combine the flour, cocoa powder, yeast, and salt. With the mixer on low speed, gradually add the filtered water until a shaggy dough forms.

Increase the mixer speed to medium and knead the dough until it is smooth and elastic, 8 to 10 minutes. Cover the bowl with a damp tea towel and let the dough rise in a warm, dry place until doubled in size, 1 hour.

On a lightly floured surface, roll out about four-fifths of the risen dough (about 14 ounces [400g]) into a thin circle about 1/16 inch (2mm) thick. Place the dough on a pizza baking pan. Fill a piping bag fitted with a ½-inch (13-mm) round tip (such as a Wilton 1A) with Nutella and pipe it ½ inch (1.3cm) from the edge. Add small pieces of chocolate along the Nutella line, then fold the dough edges over and seal tightly. Cover the pizza loosely with plastic wrap or a damp tea towel and let it proof in a warm spot for 30 minutes.

Preheat the oven to 350°F (175°C).

Bake the pizza until the crust is set and slightly crispy, about 15 minutes.

ASSEMBLE THE NAUGHTY HAZELNUT COCOA PIZZA

Right out of the oven, slather the crust with a thick layer of hazelnut praline paste. Top with a generous mix of raspberries, strawberries, blueberries, and blackberries. Fill two piping bags fitted with ⅜-inch (10-mm) round tips—one with white chocolate Chantilly cream, the other with milk chocolate. Pipe dollops over the berries, then finish with a sprinkle of crushed roasted hazelnuts. Time to slice and surrender.

What's better than a love triangle? A dessert triangle. Chocolate, vanilla, and strawberry layered together in a symphony of sticky-sweet passion. Sink your teeth in, and you'll realize why ménage à trois isn't just for French romance novels. This recipe is all about being hands-on. Just a saucepan, a wooden spoon, and a little finesse are all you need to make these layers sing.

Neapolitan Love Affair Rice Crispy Squares

 MAKES 24 SQUARES

FOR THE CHOCOLATE LAYER

5½ cups (150g) marshmallows

3½ tablespoons unsalted butter

½ cup (90g) roughly chopped dark chocolate

4½ cups (130g) crisp rice cereal (such as Rice Krispies)

FOR THE VANILLA LAYER

5½ cups (150g) marshmallows

3½ tablespoons unsalted butter

2 teaspoons pure vanilla extract

4½ cups (130g) crisp rice cereal (such as Rice Krispies)

FOR THE STRAWBERRY LAYER

5½ cups (150g) marshmallows

3½ tablespoons unsalted butter

¾ cup (70g) freeze-dried strawberry powder

Dash of pink food dye (for vibrancy; optional)

4½ cups (130g) crisp rice cereal (such as Rice Krispies)

Whipped cream for garnish

Maraschino cherries for garnish

MAKE THE CHOCOLATE LAYER

Line a 9 by 13-inch (24 by 36-cm) baking pan with parchment paper. The parchment isn't just for convenience. Think of it as lingerie for your dessert, making everything look even sexier when it's time to serve.

In a medium saucepan, melt the marshmallows and butter over low heat, stirring slowly. Once the mixture is smooth, stir in the chopped chocolate and let it melt into a luscious, glossy liquid. Add the rice cereal and fold gently until every crispy bit is coated in chocolaty goodness. Spoon the mixture into the prepared baking pan and press it firmly and evenly with a spatula or your hands (greased, of course, no sticking allowed).

CONTINUED

Neapolitan Love Affair Rice Crispy Squares

CONTINUED

MAKE THE VANILLA LAYER

Repeat the same seductive process for the vanilla layer as for the chocolate layer. Melt the marshmallows and butter over low heat until they're smooth and velvety. Stir in the vanilla, add the rice cereal, and fold until well combined. Press this layer on top of the chocolate layer, smoothing it out evenly.

MAKE THE STRAWBERRY LAYER

In a medium saucepan, melt the marshmallows and butter over low heat, taking your time (because a rushed dessert is never a good dessert). Stir in the strawberry powder and pink food dye (if you're feeling extra playful). The mixture should blush a perfect shade of flirtatious pink. Add the rice cereal and fold it into the strawberry mixture until coated. Gently press this final layer on top of the vanilla layer, smoothing it out like the last note of a love song.

FINISH THE NEAPOLITAN LOVE AFFAIR RICE CRISPY SQUARES

Firmly press the entire baking pan to compress the layers. Think of it as giving your dessert a loving hug. Let the layers cool completely, about 30 minutes, before slicing into squares.

For extra pizzazz, top each square with a dollop of whipped cream and a maraschino cherry. Now that's what I call a love affair!

WARNING

Side effects may include swooning, blushing, and possibly proposing to your dessert.

This is a love letter written in cream, honey, and a kiss of matcha. The earthy, slightly sweet, and gently bitter notes of matcha add depth to the silky richness of the panna cotta, balancing the floral honey with a whisper of umami. It's creamy, wobbly, and just waiting for you to dive in. That honeycomb garnish? Oh, that's just there to sweeten the deal and your night.

Matcha Me, Honey

MAKES 6 TO 8 SERVINGS

FOR THE PANNA COTTA

2½ sheets (8.5g) gold gelatin, or 1¼ teaspoons powdered gelatin

2 cups (480ml) heavy cream

1 cup (240ml) whole milk

⅓ cup (115g) raw honey, plus more for drizzling

2 teaspoons high-quality Japanese matcha powder, plus more for dusting

2 teaspoons pure vanilla extract

FOR THE HONEYCOMB

1 cup (200g) sugar

⅓ cup (105g) light corn syrup

⅓ cup (80ml) water

2½ teaspoons baking soda

MAKE THE PANNA COTTA

If using gelatin sheets, soak them in cold water for 5 to 10 minutes, until they're soft and pliable. Squeeze out excess water and set them aside, like a well-prepped secret weapon. If using powdered gelatin, sprinkle it over 2 tablespoons of cold water in a small bowl and let it bloom for 5 minutes.

In a medium saucepan, combine the cream and milk and heat gently over medium-low heat until it just starts to flirt with a simmer. (No boiling—this dessert likes to take it slow.)

Stir in the honey, matcha powder, and vanilla. Whisk like you're serenading it, until the honey dissolves and the matcha blends into a dreamy green swirl.

Remove from the heat and whisk in the softened gelatin sheets or the bloomed gelatin. Make sure it dissolves completely (smooth operators only).

Pour the panna cotta mixture into 6 to 8 silicone molds, each mold should hold about 1 cup. Let cool to room temperature, then chill in the refrigerator for at least 4 hours (the wait will be worth it). The panna cotta should jiggle like it's at a disco, firm enough to hold its shape but soft enough to wobble when tempted.

CONTINUED

Matcha Me, Honey

CONTINUED

◎ ───────────────────────────────────────

MAKE THE HONEYCOMB

Line a baking sheet with parchment paper. Get ready, this part's going to get bubbly and bold.

In a medium saucepan, combine the sugar, corn syrup, and water and stir over medium heat until the sugar dissolves. Then stop stirring and let it do its thing, cooking until it turns a rich, golden amber color. Use a candy thermometer and pull the mixture off the heat at 300°F (150°C).

Quickly stir in the baking soda. The mixture will foam like it's just heard a juicy secret. Pour it onto the prepared baking sheet and let it cool completely. Once hardened, break the honeycomb into bite-size pieces. Crunchy, golden perfection.

ASSEMBLE THE MATCHA ME, HONEY

Gently remove each panna cotta from its silicone mold. (Warm the mold slightly with your hands if it's being stubborn.)

Use a fine-mesh sieve to lightly dust each panna cotta with extra matcha powder, giving it that alluring green glow. Add a drizzle of honey and a few shards of honeycomb for a dessert that's almost too gorgeous to eat. (Almost.)

WARNING

Side effects may include excessive wobble envy, spontaneous declarations of love, and an uncontrollable urge to lick the plate. Consume responsibly, or don't. Daddy won't judge.

Light as air and rich as sin, this dark chocolate soufflé is the stuff of dreams and broken hearts. It rises with dramatic flair and will have you whispering, "Please, don't deflate on me!" Finished with crème anglaise, this dessert knows it's the moment you have been waiting for.

Soufflés So Good, You'll Call Me Daddy

MAKES 6 INDIVIDUAL SOUFFLÉS

FOR THE CRÈME ANGLAISE

5 egg yolks

⅓ cup (65g) granulated sugar

2 cups (475ml) whole milk

Seeds of 1 vanilla bean, or 1 tablespoon pure vanilla extract

FOR THE SOUFFLÉS

2½ tablespoons unsalted butter, plus more for coating the ramekins

Granulated sugar for coating the ramekins

¼ cup (35g) all-purpose flour

⅓ teaspoon kosher salt

¾ cup (175g) whole milk

6 tablespoons (75g) superfine or caster sugar

4¾ ounces (135g) couverture dark chocolate, chopped

4 eggs, separated

½ teaspoon cream of tartar

Confectioners' sugar for dusting

MAKE THE CRÈME ANGLAISE

In a bowl, whisk the egg yolks and granulated sugar until pale and thick.

In a medium saucepan, heat the milk and vanilla seeds over medium heat until just boiling. Remove from the heat.

Slowly pour half the hot milk into the egg yolk mixture, whisking continuously to temper the eggs. Pour the tempered mixture back into the saucepan. Lower the heat to medium-low and cook, stirring continuously, until the mixture thickens slightly and reaches 185°F (85°C). Do not let it boil. Strain the mixture through a fine-mesh sieve into a clean bowl. Chill in the refrigerator for at least 1 hour, or until fully cooled and slightly thickened. For best results, let it chill for 2 hours before serving.

MAKE THE SOUFFLÉS

Preheat the oven to 325°F (165°C). Gather six 6-ounce/180-ml ramekins.

Melt a small amount of butter and brush it thoroughly inside each ramekin. Add granulated sugar to a ramekin, rolling it around the inside until coated evenly. Shake out the excess sugar and repeat for all ramekins.

CONTINUED

Soufflés So Good, You'll Call Me Daddy

CONTINUED

In a small bowl, combine the butter, flour, and salt and mix into a smooth paste using a fork or a silicone spatula until fully incorporated.

In a saucepan, combine the milk and 3 tablespoons (38g) of the superfine sugar and bring to a boil over medium heat. Whisk in the butter-flour paste, lower the heat, and cook, whisking continuously, until thickened and smooth, about 4 minutes. Remove from the heat and whisk in the dark chocolate until fully melted. Once the mixture is smooth, whisk in the egg yolks until incorporated.

In a stand mixer fitted with the whisk attachment, beat the egg whites and cream of tartar on medium speed until foamy. Gradually add the remaining 3 tablespoons (38g) superfine sugar while whipping, then increase the mixer speed to high and beat until stiff, glossy peaks form.

Gently fold the meringue into the chocolate base in three stages. Be delicate; this is where the soufflés get their lift, and no one likes flat soufflés. Spoon the mixture into the prepared ramekins, filling to just below the rims. Level the tops with a spatula for an even rise.

Place the ramekins on a baking sheet. Bake until the soufflés have risen dramatically but still jiggle slightly in the centers, 9 to 10 minutes.

ASSEMBLE THE SOUFFLÉS SO GOOD, YOU'LL CALL ME DADDY

Serve the soufflés immediately after baking, while they're warm, risen, and irresistible.

Dust each ramekin with confectioners' sugar and then pair each with about ⅓ cup (80ml) of crème anglaise, either poured into the center or drizzled on top.

WARNING

Side effects of this dessert include spontaneous overuse of the phrase "Oh my God" and the sudden need to call someone Daddy. Proceed with caution and a spoon.

One bite and you'll understand why I call it "bliss." With creamy coconut rice at its heart, flirty layers of vibrant ube, and mango so sweet, this dish will cause spontaneous daydreams of tropical vacations, intense cravings for second helpings, and an overwhelming urge to dance the tango with your spoon. If you've never had ube before, get ready for a treat—this purple yam, beloved in Asian desserts, has a subtly sweet, nutty, and almost vanilla-like flavor that pairs beautifully with the creamy coconut and juicy mango. Consume at your own delicious risk.

Tropical Tango Rice Bliss

MAKES 4 TO 6 SERVINGS

FOR THE COCONUT RICE

1 cup (200g) glutinous rice, soaked in water overnight

1 cup (240ml) unsweetened coconut milk

¼ cup (50g) sugar

½ teaspoon fine sea salt

FOR THE UBE LAYER (OPTIONAL, BUT RECOMMENDED)

¼ cup (70g) ube halaya or ube spread

½ teaspoon ube extract

FOR THE COCONUT SAUCE

½ cup (120ml) unsweetened coconut milk

2½ tablespoons sugar

1 teaspoon cornstarch

2 teaspoons water

2 large mangoes, peeled and sliced, for topping

Toasted unsweetened coconut flakes for garnish (optional)

Sprig of fresh mint for garnish (optional)

MAKE THE COCONUT RICE

Drain the soaked glutinous rice and rinse it thoroughly.

Line a bamboo steamer with parchment paper and place it over a pot of simmering water. Spread the rice over the bottom of the steamer and steam the rice until tender and sticky, 20 to 30 minutes.

In a small saucepan, gently warm the coconut milk, sugar, and sea salt over medium heat, stirring until the sugar dissolves. Once the rice is cooked, mix it with the coconut milk mixture until every grain is infused with creamy goodness. Set aside to let the flavors meld before adding the optional ube layer.

MAKE THE OPTIONAL UBE LAYER

In a bowl, mix the ube halaya with the ube extract for a vibrant color and intense flavor.

CONTINUED

Tropical Tango Rice Bliss

CONTINUED

MAKE THE COCONUT SAUCE

In a small saucepan, gently warm the coconut milk and sugar over medium-low heat, stirring until the sugar dissolves completely.

In a separate bowl, combine the cornstarch and water and mix to create a slurry.

Gradually add the slurry to the warm coconut milk mixture while stirring continuously. Cook until the sauce thickens slightly, 1 to 2 minutes. Remove from heat and let it cool to room temperature before using.

ASSEMBLE THE TROPICAL TANGO RICE BLISS

If using the ube layer, divide the coconut rice in half. Gently fold the ube mixture into one half, leaving the other half plain.

Place a 9-inch (23-cm) springform pan on a serving plate. If using the ube layer, add one layer of the plain coconut rice to the bottom of the pan, followed by the ube rice for a pop of color and contrast.

If skipping the ube layer, simply spread the plain coconut rice evenly over the bottom.

Remove the collar of the springform pan, and arrange the mango slices on top like a golden sunburst of sweetness. Drizzle the entire creation with the coconut sauce, letting it cascade sensually over the rice and mangoes. Garnish with toasted coconut flakes and a sprig of mint, if you're feeling fancy.

If I could bathe in chocolate, I would, but until someone builds me a cocoa-filled Jacuzzi, these chocolate bars are the next best thing. With a gooey salted caramel center, a crunchy layer of peanuts and popcorn, this is indulgence at its finest. It's a treat so luxurious it practically says, "Go ahead, spoil yourself!"

Chocolate Bar None

MAKES 6 TO 8 BARS

FOR THE SALTED CARAMEL FILLING

2 cups (400g) sugar

¾ cup (165g) unsalted butter, cubed, at room temperature

1 cup (240ml) heavy cream, at room temperature

1 teaspoon fine sea salt

FOR THE CRUSHED PEANUTS

¾ cup (90g) roasted salted peanuts

FOR THE TEMPERED CHOCOLATE BASE

14 ounces (400g) couverture milk chocolate (high-quality for proper tempering)

FOR THE POPCORN TOPPING

2 cups (50g) freshly popped popcorn, lightly salted

MAKE THE SALTED CARAMEL FILLING

In a medium saucepan, heat the sugar over medium heat, stirring continuously until it melts into a golden amber liquid. Keep an eye on it. Caramel can go from dreamy to burnt faster than a bad date. Carefully add the butter, stirring as the mixture bubbles like it's got a crush on you. Slowly pour in the cream, still stirring, and let it bubble for another minute. Remove from the heat and stir in the sea salt. Transfer the caramel to a heatproof bowl and let it cool completely before using.

MAKE THE CRUSHED PEANUTS

In a food processor, pulse the peanuts until coarsely ground. (Or, if you're feeling hands-on, crush the peanuts with a mortar and a pestle.) Leave some chunks for texture. This is a chocolate bar, not peanut butter.

MAKE THE TEMPERED CHOCOLATE BASE

Finely chop the milk chocolate and divide it into two portions: two-thirds to one-third. In a heatproof bowl set over a pot of barely simmering water (creating a double boiler), melt the larger portion, stirring continuously, until the chocolate reaches 104° to 113°F (40° to 45°C). Remove the bowl from the double boiler and gradually add the remaining one-third of the chocolate, stirring until smooth and the temperature cools to 84° to 86°F (29° to 30°C).

CONTINUED

Chocolate Bar None

CONTINUED

ASSEMBLE THE CHOCOLATE BAR NONE

Before starting, make sure you have 6 to 8 silicone chocolate bar molds and a bench scraper for smoothing the chocolate. Reserve about one-third of the tempered chocolate for sealing the bars later. If you don't have a bench scraper, an offset spatula or the back of a knife can be used instead. To prepare the base layer, pour the tempered chocolate into a silicone chocolate bar mold, tilting to coat the bottom and sides evenly. It's possible to work with multiple molds at a time—2 or 3 simultaneously is manageable, depending on workspace and speed. Flip the mold upside down onto parchment paper and scrape off any excess chocolate with the bench scraper. Let the mold rest upside down for 10 minutes to set.

Turn the mold right side up. Sprinkle a light, even layer of crushed peanuts over the partially set chocolate.

Pour a layer of cooled salted caramel into the mold, spreading it evenly. Leave a small space at the top of the mold for the final chocolate layer.

Pour the reserved tempered chocolate over the caramel layer to seal the bar. Smooth the top with a bench scraper, like the perfectionist you are.

While the chocolate is still wet, sprinkle freshly popped popcorn over the exposed surface of the mold. This will become the bottom of the finished chocolate bar once the mold is removed. The popcorn adds texture and whimsy, even if it's not fully visible in the final bar. (If you want more visual pop, feel free to press in a few whole pieces after removing the mold for presentation.)

Let the bars set at room temperature for 20 minutes, then transfer them to the fridge for an additional 10 minutes to fully solidify.

Once the bars are completely set, gently pop them out of the molds.

WARNING

Consuming this chocolate bar may result in an uncontrollable desire to bathe in caramel, rename your cat "Cocoa," or claim popcorn as a health food. Proceed with delicious caution.

If mountains looked this good, I'd be climbing them every day—no ropes, no gear, just pure, delicious determination. With a base of rich chocolate cake, a creamy pistachio spread, and a swirled meringue finish that is torched to golden perfection, the Alpine Affair Cakes will have you scaling new heights of indulgence. Pack your fork as we're going on an edible expedition.

Alpine Affair Cakes

MAKES 4 TO 6 SERVINGS

FOR THE CHOCOLATE CAKES

1½ cups (210g) all-purpose flour

½ cup (40g) unsweetened Dutch-processed cocoa powder

1 teaspoon baking powder

1 teaspoon baking soda

½ teaspoon kosher salt

1½ cups (300g) sugar

2 eggs

¾ cup (175ml) whole milk

⅓ cup (80ml) vegetable oil

1½ teaspoons pure vanilla extract

¾ cup (175ml) boiling water

FOR THE PISTACHIO SPREAD

1 cup (140g) shelled unsalted pistachios

½ teaspoon kosher salt (optional)

FOR THE MERINGUE

4 egg whites

½ teaspoon cream of tartar

1¼ cups (250g) sugar

½ cup (60g) chopped unsalted pistachios for sprinkling

MAKE THE CHOCOLATE CAKES

Preheat the oven to 350°F (175°C). Line a large rimmed baking sheet (about 10 by 15 inches [25 by 38cm]) or an 8-inch (20-cm) round cake pan with parchment paper.

Into a large bowl, sift together the flour, cocoa powder, baking powder, baking soda, and salt. Stir in the sugar.

In another bowl, whisk together the eggs, milk, oil, and vanilla until smooth. Gradually add the mixture to the flour mixture, stirring gently. Whisk in the boiling water a little at a time until the batter is smooth and slightly thin.

Pour the batter into the prepared baking sheet or pan. Bake until a toothpick inserted into the center comes out clean, 20 to 25 minutes if using a baking sheet or 25 to 30 minutes if using a cake pan.

Let the cake cool in the pan for 10 minutes, then carefully invert it onto a wire rack and remove the pan. Gently peel away the parchment paper. Allow the cake to cool completely before

CONTINUED

Alpine Affair Cakes

CONTINUED

cutting out the individual bases. If the cake is too warm, it may crumble when cut. Use a 3-inch (7.5-cm) round cutter to cut out four to six individual cake bases from the cooled cake.

MAKE THE PISTACHIO SPREAD

In a small dry skillet, toast the pistachios over medium heat for 5 minutes to enhance their flavor. Cool before blending. In a food processor, pulse the pistachios until they form a smooth paste. Scrape down the sides as needed. Add salt (if using).

MAKE THE MERINGUE

In the clean, grease-free bowl of a stand mixer fitted with the whisk attachment, beat the egg whites and cream of tartar on medium speed until soft peaks form, 2 to 3 minutes. Increase the mixer speed to high and slowly add the sugar, 1 tablespoon at a time, until stiff, glossy peaks form. The meringue should hold its shape and feel silky, not grainy.

ASSEMBLE THE ALPINE AFFAIR CAKES

Spread a generous layer of pistachio spread over each chocolate cake round. Sprinkle each with crushed pistachios for added crunch.

Fill a piping bag fitted with a star tip (#4B or #6B or 12- or 13-mm diameter) with the meringue and pipe it onto each cake in a spiral motion, starting at the base and working upward to cover the top.

Use a kitchen torch to toast the meringue until golden brown, giving your mini mountains a warm, caramelized finish.

Watch as your guests cut into these showstopping mini mountains and "peak" into uncontrolled admiration.

Welcome to Almond Lovers Anonymous, where the first step is admitting you have a problem, and that problem is not having enough of these luscious almond-chocolate logs in your life. These logs may cause an irresistible urge to hoard them from family members. Made with rich marzipan, a kiss of lemon zest, and a glossy chocolate glaze, these treats are so addictive they'll have you raising your hand and saying, "Hi, my name is [your name], and I ate the whole batch."

Almond Lovers Anonymous Logs

MAKES ABOUT 25 LOGS

FOR THE LOGS

5 ounces (140g) raw marzipan

1 egg plus 1 egg yolk

½ cup (60g) almond flour

Finely grated zest of 1 lemon

FOR THE GLAZE

12 ounces (340g) semisweet chocolate, chopped

2 tablespoons cocoa butter, finely chopped

½ cup (60g) sliced almonds for sprinkling

Confectioners' sugar for sprinkling

MAKE THE LOGS

Preheat the oven to 350°F (175°C). Lightly grease a silicone éclair mold (or two, depending on your mold—you should aim for around 24 cavities in total) or line with parchment strips—because these logs deserve a little elegance.

In the bowl of a stand mixer fitted with the paddle attachment, combine the marzipan, egg, egg yolk, almond flour, and lemon zest and mix on medium speed until they form a smooth paste. Don't be surprised if you're tempted to sneak a taste.

Fill a piping bag fitted with a plain ½-inch (1.3-cm) tip with the marzipan paste. Pipe long, even lines of the mixture onto the prepared mold, filling each one evenly. No need to leave space—they'll stay delightfully in line. Bake until the logs are firm to the touch, about 10 minutes. Let cool completely on the baking sheet.

MAKE THE GLAZE

In a heatproof bowl, combine the semisweet chocolate and cocoa butter and place the bowl over a pot with barely simmering water. Stir occasionally until the chocolate is smooth and glossy. The cocoa butter thins the chocolate to make dipping an absolute breeze.

ASSEMBLE THE ALMOND LOVERS ANONYMOUS LOGS

Using two forks, dip the ends of each log into the melted chocolate, ensuring the ends are fully coated. Lift it out and let the excess drip off into the bowl. Place the dipped logs on a wire rack and generously sprinkle with slivered almonds while the chocolate is still wet. Let them sit at room temperature until the chocolate hardens and then sprinkle with the confectioners' sugar.

Regular truffles just won't cut it after these sultry little bites. They are smooth, boozy, and dusted in cocoa like they're strutting down a dessert runway. These truffles get their lusciously smooth, melt-in-your-mouth texture thanks to glucose syrup, which prevents sugar crystallization and keeps the ganache rich and creamy. They do come with a warning though: Serving these may lead to repeated requests, sudden declarations of love, and the occasional fight over the last one. You may even find yourself truffle hoarding and having the uncontrollable urge to declare these as your one true love.

Black Raspberry Rendezvous Truffles

MAKES ABOUT 60 TRUFFLES

FOR THE TRUFFLES

1¼ pounds (570g) milk chocolate, finely chopped

12 ounces (340g) bittersweet chocolate, finely chopped

1 tablespoon glucose syrup

2 cups (475ml) heavy cream

¼ cup plus 2 tablespoons (90ml) black raspberry liqueur

2 tablespoons unsalted butter, softened

FOR THE FINISHING TOUCH

1¼ cups (100g) unsweetened Dutch-processed cocoa powder

⅓ cup (40g) confectioners' sugar

MAKE THE TRUFFLES

In the top of a double boiler over barely simmering water, combine the milk chocolate, bittersweet chocolate, glucose syrup, and cream and stir gently and lovingly until smooth and shiny. Remove from the heat and stir in the black raspberry liqueur and softened butter until the mixture is velvety and irresistible.

Pour the mixture into a shallow 8-inch (20-cm) square baking dish or a small rimmed tray. Cover with plastic wrap, pressing the plastic gently against the surface to keep things smooth (no one likes a skin here). Chill in the refrigerator until firm, 2 to 4 hours.

Line a baking sheet with parchment paper. Using your hands or a small scoop, take teaspoon-size portions of the chilled mixture and roll them into balls. Daddy's tip: Coat your hands with cocoa powder if the chocolate gets too clingy. Place the rolled truffles on the prepared baking sheet and chill in the refrigerator to firm up, 30 minutes.

MAKE THE FINISHING TOUCH & ASSEMBLE

Into a bowl, sift the cocoa powder and confectioners' sugar, blending them into a silky-smooth dusting mixture.

Roll each truffle in the cocoa-sugar mixture until fully coated, place on a baking sheet, and let them set at room temperature for 10 minutes before chilling in the refrigerator until solid, about an hour. Serve cold.

Let me introduce you to the ice cream that'll steal the spotlight during any intimate tête-à-tête. This Burnt Vanilla Ice Cream is dramatic and just mysterious enough to make your date lean in for another scoop. The charred vanilla brings a smoky, sultry edge, and if you're feeling bold, that activated charcoal adds a flair so daring it might just text you at 2 a.m. Once you whip this up, your freezer might become the most seductive place in your kitchen.

Burnt Vanilla Ice Cream

MAKES ABOUT 1 PINT (2 CUPS/480ML) OR 4 SMALL SERVINGS

1 vanilla bean, split

1 cup (240ml) heavy cream

½ cup (120ml) whole milk

½ cup (100g) sugar

2 egg yolks

1 teaspoon activated charcoal powder (for dramatic flair; optional)

Store-bought chocolate sauce for garnish

Store-bought cookies, crushed, for garnish

In a medium saucepan, heat the split vanilla bean over medium heat until slightly charred. Scrape the seeds into the pan and discard the vanilla bean pod. Add the cream, milk, and sugar and heat until steaming but not boiling. Remove from the heat and let the mixture steep for 10 minutes.

In a mixing bowl, whisk the egg yolks until pale and slightly thickened. Gradually whisk in the hot cream mixture, then return the mixture to the saucepan. Cook over medium heat, stirring continuously, until the custard coats the back of a spoon, reaching a temperature of 175°F (80°C). Strain everything into a bowl through a fine-mesh sieve. Stir in the activated charcoal for drama (if using) and chill the custard in the refrigerator for at least 4 hours.

Transfer the chilled custard to an ice-cream machine and churn according to the manufacturer's directions until firm. Spoon onto individual plates, garnish with chocolate sauce and crushed cookies to serve.

Let me set the scene: candlelight, a slow jazz playlist, and a plate of these strawberries glistening like they just stepped off the cover of *GQ*. They're not just dipped in chocolate; they're dipped in seduction. Each bite is a tuxedo-clad invitation to throw caution to the wind. They're classy, they're decadent, and they know they look good. Just like me. Because this recipe is all about presentation, be sure to invest in high-quality chocolate so you get beautiful results. Grab your strawberries and let's get these dashing little devils ready for their red-carpet debut.

Tuxedo Strawberries

MAKES 12 STRAWBERRIES

4 ounces (115g) white chocolate (you deserve the good stuff; don't settle for less), chopped

1 teaspoon coconut oil or vegetable shortening (it makes the chocolate smoother than a slow dance; optional)

12 large fresh strawberries, washed and thoroughly dried (wet strawberries are a chocolate disaster waiting to happen, so don't skimp here)

4 ounces (115g) dark chocolate, chopped (as dark and mysterious as a Donut Daddy nightcap)

Grab a microwavable bowl and toss in the white chocolate. Microwave in 20-second bursts, stirring between rounds, until the white chocolate is melted and silky. Think of it like foreplay: Low and slow, baby, we're not in a rush. If it's too thick, stir in ½ teaspoon of the coconut oil (if using) to loosen things up.

Line a baking sheet with parchment paper. Hold each strawberry by the stem and dip it into the melted white chocolate, swirling it around for full coverage. Let any excess drip off like it's shy. Place the dipped strawberries on the prepared baking sheet. Let them sit until the chocolate sets, 15 to 20 minutes.

Now it's time to bring the drama. In a microwavable bowl, melt the dark chocolate as you did the white chocolate: in the microwave in 20-second bursts, stirring between rounds. Add the remaining ½ teaspoon coconut oil (if using); smooth chocolate is nonnegotiable.

Once the white chocolate has set, dip each strawberry into the dark chocolate at a slight angle, covering one side. Then tilt the strawberry the other way to create a *V* shape, leaving a cheeky little triangle of white chocolate in the middle. This is the tuxedo moment. Place the strawberries back on the parchment and let them set.

Use a toothpick or a piping bag fitted with a fine tip to dot dark chocolate "buttons" down the white chocolate shirt.

Let the tuxedo strawberries set at room temperature, or chill briefly in the refrigerator if you're in a hurry. Once set, arrange on a platter and get ready for jaws to drop.

03

Dangerously
Decadent
Desserts

Sophisticated Sweets Crafted to Captivate Every Craving

My sugar-starved sweethearts, you've arrived at the most scandalous chapter of this cookbook: Dangerously Decadent Desserts. This is where desserts stop being polite and start getting downright filthy but sophisticated. You're about to enter a world of buttery layers, silky creams, and enough caramel to satisfy your wildest dreams. These recipes are sweet, sexy, and just a little chaotic, basically me in dessert form. I know you need a moment to collect yourself—maybe sit down, fan your face?

Well, my dear, are you ready? Good. Now turn the page and let's bake like the world's watching.

Listen closely, my sweet-toothed tempters: This isn't your nonna's tiramisu. Oh no, this creation is a seduction in strawberry form. Think juicy strawberry jelly, impossibly light mascarpone cream, and delicate ladyfingers. The layers come together in a dessert that's as smooth as my pickup lines and just as irresistible. The strawberries will glisten, the mascarpone cream will beg to be swirled, and by the time you're layering it all together, you might need a moment to cool down (and maybe a glass of wine).

Berry Naughty Layers Strawberry Tiramisu

 MAKES 8 TO 10 SERVINGS

FOR THE STRAWBERRY JELLY

2 cups (500g) strawberry puree

½ cup (100g) sugar

¼ cup (60ml) cold water

2 teaspoons gelatin powder

FOR THE CREAMY TOPPING

1¼ cups (300ml) heavy cream

1 cup (225g) mascarpone cheese

2 tablespoons sugar

FOR THE TIRAMISU

3 ounces (85g) sweet Marsala wine or brewed espresso coffee

2 to 3 tablespoons simple syrup

2½ to 3 cups (600 to 720g) mascarpone cream, homemade (see page 205) or store-bought

24 to 30 ladyfingers, homemade (see page 200) or store-bought

Freeze-dried strawberry powder for garnish

Quartered fresh strawberries for garnish

Edible gold leaf for garnish

MAKE THE STRAWBERRY JELLY

In a mixing bowl, combine the strawberry puree and sugar, stirring until the sugar dissolves. Give it a little taste, because you deserve a preview of what's to come.

In a separate bowl, add the cold water and sprinkle the gelatin over it. Let the mixture sit for 5 minutes to bloom. It should look like it's having a little spa day (soft and plump).

In a saucepan, gently heat the bloomed gelatin over low heat until it's fully melted. Stir it into the strawberry mixture like you're introducing two lovers at a candlelit dinner. Smooth, slow, sensual.

Line a rimmed baking sheet or a 9-inch (23-cm) square mold with parchment paper. Pour the strawberry mixture onto the baking sheet, spreading it evenly. Slide it into the fridge and let it chill for 2 hours. Patience, darling. The best things come to those who wait.

CONTINUED

Berry Naughty Layers Strawberry Tiramisu

CONTINUED

MAKE THE CREAMY TOPPING

In a mixing bowl, combine the cream, mascarpone, and sugar and whip with a handheld electric mixer until stiff peaks form, 4 to 5 minutes.

Fill a piping bag fitted with your favorite decorative tip (because we love a little flair) with the creamy topping.

ASSEMBLE THE BERRY NAUGHTY LAYERS STRAWBERRY TIRAMISU

Have ready a 9-inch (23-cm) square serving dish.

In a small bowl, whisk together the Marsala and simple syrup until fully combined.

Fill another piping bag fitted with a ½-inch (12- or 13-mm) round tip with the mascarpone cream. Be sure to distinguish between the mascarpone cream used for layering and the creamy topping used for decoration, as both play different roles in the final dessert.

Arrange a layer of ladyfingers in the serving dish, brushing them generously with the Marsala mixture. Pipe a layer of mascarpone cream on top. Spread on a layer of strawberry jelly. Repeat the layering, adding ladyfingers, mascarpone cream, and another layer of jelly.

Finish with a thick, even layer of mascarpone cream. Use the creamy topping to pipe your most flirtatious designs on top.

Get fancy: Dust with strawberry powder, tuck in strawberry quarters, and add edible gold leaf. It's glamorous, it's decadent, and it's so extra.

Chill in the refrigerator for at least 4 hours, or overnight if you can resist temptation, before serving.

This is the flaky affair you've been waiting for. Are you ready to get your hands buttery? More than a pastry, these are a love affair wrapped in golden, flaky layers. Making them is a labor of love, but trust me, when you pull these beauties out of the oven, all puffed up and golden like they've spent the day basking on the Riviera, you'll know it was worth every roll and fold. Biting into one might awaken desires you didn't know you had.

Golden Indulgence Croissants

MAKES 12 TO 16 CROISSANTS

4 cups (560g) all-purpose flour	4 teaspoons fine sea salt	1¾ cups (415ml) water
½ cup (100g) sugar	4 teaspoons instant dry yeast	1 egg
2 tablespoons whole milk	2¼ cups (495g) unsalted butter, softened	

In the bowl of a stand mixer fitted with the dough hook, combine the flour, sugar, 1 tablespoon of the milk, the sea salt, yeast, ¼ cup (55g) of the softened butter, and the water and mix on low speed until fully incorporated, 2 to 3 minutes.

Increase the mixer speed to medium-high and knead the dough until it is elastic, 8 to 9 minutes. The dough should pass the windowpane test (see page 20) but still break slightly.

Shape the dough into a ball, flatten it slightly, and place it on a lightly floured surface. Wrap it loosely in plastic wrap to prevent drying. Let the dough rest in a warm, dry place for 2 hours (or 1 hour if room temperature is above 70°F [21°C]). During this time, the dough will start to form small bubbles and puff up slightly, but it should not double in size.

Chill the rested dough in the refrigerator until it is cold and firm, about 30 minutes. The dough and the prepared butter block (below) should be at a similar consistency—cold but pliable—for successful lamination.

Place the remaining 2 cups (440g) butter between two sheets of parchment paper and roll into a precise 12 by 8-inch (30 by 20-cm) rectangle. Chill until firm but pliable.

On a lightly floured surface, roll the dough into an approximate 12 by 18-inch (30 by 45-cm) rectangle. Place the butter rectangle on top and fold the dough in half to completely seal the butter.

CONTINUED

Golden Indulgence Croissants

Roll the dough into a rectangle about ⅜ inch (8 to 9mm) thick. Perform a letter fold (one-third of the dough folded in, then the opposite third over it). Wrap the folded dough in plastic wrap and chill in the refrigerator for 30 to 45 minutes.

Repeat the process—rolling, folding, and chilling—two more times for a total of three letter folds.

Line a rimmed baking sheet with parchment paper and set aside.

After the final fold, roll the dough to a thickness of ⅛ inch (3mm). Trim the edges for clean lines and cut into triangles with a base width of 3½ inches (9cm) and a height of about 7 inches (18cm).

Make a small slit at the base of each triangle to help with rolling. Roll tightly from base to tip, stretching the dough slightly as you go. Place the rolled triangles on the prepared baking sheet with the tips tucked underneath.

Cover the croissants loosely with plastic wrap or a damp tea towel and let them proof at room temperature until they are puffy but not overproofed (when the dough looks too swollen, jiggles excessively, and collapses when touched), 2 hours.

Preheat the oven to 375°F (190°C).

In a small bowl, whisk the egg and the remaining 1 tablespoon milk until combined for the egg wash. Brush the egg wash over the croissants for a golden finish.

Bake until puffed and gloriously golden, 20 to 25 minutes. Cool slightly on a wire rack, then enjoy!

Is it possible for a dessert to flirt with me?

I looked up from the glossy tart in front of me, passion fruit cream shimmering under the light, with perfect meringue peaks. If this tart doesn't make you blush, nothing will!

Here's the thing: It's not just a dessert, it's an experience. It seduces you, one layer at a time, until you're left helpless, wondering how something so simple could feel so . . . intimate. And it all starts with pâte sablée, a French short-crust dough with a buttery, melt-in-your-mouth texture. Unlike pâte sucrée, which is crisp, or pâte brisée, which is flaky, this dough is tender and delicate—perfect for creamy fillings. So grab your whisk, your tart pan, and your sass.

Passion Fruit Tart of Temptation

MAKES 8 TO 10 SERVINGS

FOR THE PÂTE SABLÉE

1 cup (140g) all-purpose flour

½ cup (60g) confectioners' sugar

¼ teaspoon kosher salt

½ cup (110g) cold unsalted butter, cubed

1 egg

1 teaspoon pure vanilla extract

FOR THE PASSION FRUIT CREAM

2 sheets (6.8g) gold gelatin

1 cup (200g) superfine or caster sugar

2 teaspoons freshly grated lemon zest (about 2 lemons)

½ cup (130g) passion fruit puree

4 eggs

½ cup (110g) unsalted butter, cubed, at room temperature

FOR THE RASPBERRY GEL

2½ sheets (8.5g) gold gelatin

2 cups (240g) fresh or frozen raspberries

¼ cup (50g) granulated sugar

1 tablespoon freshly squeezed lemon juice

⅓ cup plus 1 tablespoon (95ml) room-temperature water

FOR THE WHITE CHOCOLATE DISK

1 cup plus 2 tablespoons (200g) chopped white chocolate

FOR THE MERINGUE TOPPING

⅓ cup (110ml) egg whites (from 3 eggs)

½ cup (100g) granulated sugar

¾ cup (90g) confectioners' sugar, sifted

MAKE THE PÂTE SABLÉE

In the bowl of a stand mixer fitted with the paddle attachment, combine the flour, confectioners' sugar, and salt and mix on low speed just to evenly distribute the ingredients, 10 to 15 seconds.

Add the cubed butter and rub it in with your fingertips or a bench scraper until the mixture resembles coarse crumbs. It should feel like running sand through your hands on a warm beach.

CONTINUED

Passion Fruit Tart of Temptation

(If you want to use the mixer, mix on low speed until the mixture resembles coarse crumbs, 1 to 2 minutes.)

Add the egg and vanilla and mix until the dough just begins to come together, 30 seconds to 1 minute. If it's a little dry, add a teaspoon of cold water, but don't overdo it.

Shape the dough into a disk on a lightly floured surface, wrap it tightly in plastic wrap, and let it chill in the fridge for at least 30 minutes. It needs time to firm up and become fabulous.

Preheat the oven to 350°F (175°C). Line a 9-inch (23-cm) tart pan with parchment paper.

On a lightly floured surface, roll out the dough to about ⅛ inch (3mm) thick. Press it into the bottom and sides of the tart pan. Line the tart shell with parchment paper, then add pie weights.

Bake for 15 minutes. Remove the weights and the parchment, and bake until golden brown, another 5 to 10 minutes. Let it cool completely.

MAKE THE PASSION FRUIT CREAM

Soak the gelatin sheets in cold water until softened, about 5 minutes. Drain and set aside.

Get steamy. In a medium saucepan, whisk together the superfine sugar, lemon zest, passion fruit puree, and eggs over low heat. Cook gently, stirring continuously, until the mixture thickens and reaches 170°F (75°C). Think silky, not scrambled.

Remove from the heat and stir in the softened gelatin until fully dissolved. Strain the mixture into a bowl through a fine-mesh sieve to remove the zest for a smooth, seductive finish.

Butter it up. When the mixture has cooled to about 130°F (55°C), whisk in the butter, one cube at a time, until the cream is smooth and luscious. Pour the cream into a heatproof container, cover it, and chill in the refrigerator until set, 2 to 3 hours.

MAKE THE RASPBERRY GEL

Soak the gelatin sheets in cold water until softened, about 5 minutes. Drain and set aside.

In a medium saucepan, combine the raspberries, granulated sugar, lemon juice, and water. Simmer gently on medium heat until the raspberries break down into a jammy consistency.

Strain the mixture to remove the seeds, leaving behind a smooth, vibrant mixture.

Stir the softened gelatin into the warm raspberry mixture until dissolved, about 5 minutes. Pour the gel into a heatproof container, cover it, and chill in the refrigerator until set, 2 to 3 hours.

MAKE THE WHITE CHOCOLATE DISK

In the top of a double boiler over barely simmering water, melt the white chocolate to 113°F (45°C). Remove from the heat and let it cool to 78°F (27°C), then warm again slightly to 84° to 86°F (29° to 30°C) for perfect tempering.

On a sheet of parchment paper, trace a circle using your 9-inch (23-cm) tart pan. Pour the white chocolate into the center of the traced circle and spread it evenly to reach the edges of the circle. Once the white chocolate is partially firm, use a 6-inch (15-cm) tart ring to cut a ring. Let it set until fully firm, discarding the center.

MAKE THE MERINGUE TOPPING

In a heatproof bowl set over a double boiler, whisk together the egg whites and granulated sugar. Whisk continuously until the sugar dissolves and the mixture reaches 122°F (50°C). You can test this by rubbing a bit of the mixture between your fingers—if it feels smooth (no sugar granules), it's ready.

Remove from the heat and whisk with a handheld electric mixer until stiff peaks form, 4 to 5 minutes. Fold in the confectioners' sugar for that extra sweetness.

ASSEMBLE THE PASSION FRUIT TART OF TEMPTATION

To make the base layer, spread the chilled passion fruit cream evenly across the baked tart shell. Smooth it like you mean it.

Fill a piping bag fitted with a star tip with the meringue topping. Pipe decorative patterns over the passion fruit cream, leaving the center exposed.

Place the white chocolate disk gently on top, aligning it perfectly with the edges of the tart.

If desired, pipe additional meringue into the center of the white chocolate disk, creating height and drama.

Fill another piping bag fitted with a small round tip with the chilled raspberry gel. Artfully pipe raspberry balls around the edge of the tart or on the meringue for pops of color.

Chill the tart for 2 to 3 hours in the refrigerator until firm, slice carefully, and serve cold.

What happens when spicy cardamom, zesty orange, and velvety coffee ice cream come together? Chaos, but the good kind, the kind where every bite is a flavor riot in your mouth. Top it off with crunchy, sweet amaretti cookies, and suddenly, you're spooning like it's your first date all over again. This dessert might just steal the show and your heart.

Cardamom and Chaos Ice Cream

MAKES 6 TO 8 SERVINGS

⅔ cup (160ml) whole milk

1 cup plus 2 tablespoons (265ml) heavy cream

1¼ cups (300ml) whipping cream (for extra richness; optional)

2 tablespoons light corn syrup or honey

½ cup (100g) sugar

1 teaspoon ground cardamom, or 6 to 8 green cardamom pods

1 tablespoon finely ground coffee beans, or 2 teaspoons instant coffee powder

1 tablespoon freshly grated orange zest

1 teaspoon cornstarch

Pinch of kosher salt

2 egg yolks

½ cup crushed amaretti cookies, homemade (see page 216) or store-bought

In a large saucepan, combine the milk, cream, whipping cream (if using), corn syrup, and ¼ cup (50g) of the sugar. Stir in the cardamom (Daddy's tip: If you're using whole cardamom pods, lightly crush the cardamom before steeping to release their flavor. Remember to strain them out!), ground coffee, and orange zest. Heat gently over medium heat, stirring occasionally, until hot but not boiling. Remove from the heat, cover, and let the mixture steep for 30 minutes to allow the flavors to infuse the dairy.

In a small bowl, combine the remaining ¼ cup (50g) sugar, the cornstarch, and salt and mix well to prevent lumps when added later.

Strain the infused milk mixture through a fine-mesh sieve into a clean saucepan to remove the solids. Place the saucepan over medium heat and gradually whisk in the sugar mixture until fully dissolved.

In a separate bowl, lightly beat the egg yolks with a whisk. Slowly pour a ladle of the hot milk mixture into the egg yolks, whisking continuously to temper them (preventing scrambled eggs). Pour the tempered egg yolks back into the saucepan, stirring continuously. Cook the mixture over medium-low heat, stirring continuously, until it thickens slightly and coats the back of a spoon, 5 to 7 minutes. Do not let the mixture boil.

CONTINUED

Cardamom and Chaos Ice Cream

CONTINUED

Remove from the heat and pour the custard through the fine-mesh sieve into a clean bowl. Let cool for 30 minutes at room temperature. Cover the custard with plastic wrap pressed directly onto the surface to prevent a skin from forming. Chill in the refrigerator for at least 6 hours or overnight.

Pour the chilled custard into your ice-cream maker and churn according to the manufacturer's instructions until it reaches a soft-serve consistency, typically 20 to 30 minutes.

Transfer the churned ice cream to a freezer-safe container. Press parchment paper or plastic wrap onto the surface, cover with a lid, and freeze for at least 4 hours.

Serve the Chaos. Scoop the ice cream into bowls or cones. Crush or crumble the amaretti cookies on top for a delightful crunch.

With these éclairs, we're dialing up the decadence and adding a touch of "naughty" charm. Think classic French pastry with an Irish twist, and enough whimsy to leave your guests giggling between bites. Oh, and don't blame me if your dessert table becomes a battlefield of adoration. Overconsumption may lead to unbuttoned pants, joyful tears, and the uncontrollable urge to Instagram your masterpiece with hashtags like #ÉclairGasm and #DonutDaddyMadeMeDoIt. Remember: I warned you! (P.S. This recipe uses a decorative transfer sheet—thin plastic with cocoa butter designs that imprint onto chocolate as it sets.)

Éclair–iously Intoxicating

MAKES 10 TO 12 ÉCLAIRS

FOR THE BAILEYS MILK CHOCOLATE MOUSSE

½ sheet (1.7g) gold gelatin

1 cup (240ml) chopped milk chocolate

1½ cups (360ml) heavy cream

2 teaspoons glucose syrup

¼ cup plus 2 teaspoons (70ml) Baileys Original Irish Cream (adjust if you're feeling particularly cheeky)

FOR THE COCOA SABLAGE TOPPING

3½ tablespoons (50g) unsalted butter, softened

¼ cup plus 2 tablespoons (50g) all-purpose flour

¼ cup (50g) packed dark brown sugar

1 tablespoon Dutch-processed cocoa powder

Pinch of kosher salt

FOR THE CHOUX PASTRY

½ cup (120ml) water

½ cup (120ml) whole milk

½ cup (110g) unsalted butter, cubed

1 teaspoon granulated sugar

¼ teaspoon kosher salt

1 cup (140g) all-purpose flour

4 eggs

FOR THE CHOCOLATE DISKS

1 cup (180g) chopped couverture dark chocolate

FOR THE WHIPPED CHOCOLATE CHANTILLY CREAM

¾ cup plus 1 tablespoon (190ml) heavy cream, chilled

1 tablespoon confectioners' sugar

1 tablespoon Dutch-processed cocoa powder, plus more for dusting

Chocolate curls for garnish

MAKE THE BAILEYS MILK CHOCOLATE MOUSSE

Soak the gelatin sheets in cold water until softened, 5 minutes. Drain and set aside.

In the top of a double boiler over barely simmering water, melt the milk chocolate until glossy and smooth, a little like Donut Daddy's winks.

In a small saucepan, gently heat ¾ cup (180ml) of the cream and the glucose, stirring until the glucose dissolves. No boiling—let's keep it sensual, not aggressive.

CONTINUED

Éclair-iously Intoxicating

Stir the softened gelatin into the warm cream mixture until it's one velvety entity. Slowly introduce this mixture to your melted milk chocolate, stirring until you can see your reflection in its glossy surface. Blend in the Baileys, letting the aroma make your kitchen smell like a chocolatier's dream.

In the bowl of a stand mixer fitted with the paddle attachment, whip the remaining ¾ cup (180ml) cream on medium-low speed until soft peaks whisper sweet nothings, 2 to 3 minutes. Fold the whipped cream into the chocolate mixture in loving batches until combined.

Transfer the mousse to a clean bowl and press plastic wrap directly onto the surface to prevent a skin from forming. Chill in the refrigerator for at least 4 hours, or until the mousse is as firm and indulgent as your resolve not to share. Wash and dry the mixer bowl before proceeding with the cocoa sablage topping.

MAKE THE COCOA SABLAGE TOPPING

In the bowl of the stand mixer fitted with the paddle attachment, combine the butter, flour, brown sugar, cocoa powder, and salt and mix on low speed until smooth, like cocoa-flavored silk.

Roll the cocoa dough between two sheets of parchment paper to a ¹⁄₁₆-inch (1.5- to 2-mm) thickness—this is your sablage runway. Freeze until firm, about 30 minutes.

Cut the sablage using a 1½- to 2-inch (4- to 5-cm) tart ring. Return to the freezer until it's time to crown your choux. Wash and dry the mixer bowl before proceeding with choux pastry.

MAKE THE CHOUX PASTRY

In a medium saucepan, combine the water, milk, butter, granulated sugar, and salt and cook over medium heat until the butter melts and the mixture begins to boil gently.

Lower the heat to low. Add the flour all at once and stir vigorously with a wooden spoon or spatula. Continue stirring until the dough comes together into a ball and a thin film forms on the bottom of the pan, 2 to 3 minutes.

Transfer the dough to the bowl of the stand mixer fitted with the paddle attachment and mix on low to release steam and cool slightly, 2 to 3 minutes. The dough should still be warm but not hot enough to scramble the eggs.

Add the eggs, one at a time, beating well after each addition. The dough should become smooth, glossy, and pipable. To check the consistency, scoop up some dough with a spatula—it should form a *V* shape as it drops back into the bowl.

Line a baking sheet with parchment paper. Fill a piping bag fitted with a large round or French star tip with the dough and pipe the dough into 6-inch (15-cm) lengths onto the prepared

CONTINUED

baking sheet. Leave space between the éclairs as they will puff up. Freeze the piped choux dough until firm, about 30 minutes.

Lay your precut sablage on top of the frozen piped dough, a couture coat for your pastry.

Bake at 300°F (150°C) for 20 minutes, then increase the oven temperature to 325°F (165°C) and bake until golden and puffed, another 15 to 18 minutes. Lower the oven temperature to 275°F (135°C) and dry the éclairs for 8 to 10 minutes to set the structure and prevent sogginess. It's a stage of rising and golden transformations.

MAKE THE CHOCOLATE DISKS

In the top of a double boiler over barely simmering water or in a microwave in 30-second bursts, melt the chocolate to 113°F (45°C), stirring frequently. Let the chocolate cool to 81°F (27°C) while continuing to stir. Gently reheat to 88°F (31°C) for proper tempering. The chocolate should be smooth, glossy, and ready to work with.

Spread the tempered chocolate evenly over a decorative transfer sheet using an offset spatula. Aim for a thin, uniform layer that will set cleanly. Let the chocolate set slightly but remain pliable.

While the chocolate is semiset, use a 6 by 2-inch (15 by 5-cm) tart ring to cut out chocolate disks. Leave the disks to fully set and harden before peeling them off the transfer sheet and using them to crown your éclairs.

MAKE THE WHIPPED CHOCOLATE CHANTILLY CREAM

Chill a mixer bowl in the freezer for 10 to 15 minutes.

In the chilled mixer bowl, combine the cream, confectioners' sugar, and cocoa powder. Using a whisk or the stand mixer with the whisk attachment, whip the mixture on medium-high speed until stiff peaks form, 4 to 5 minutes. Be careful not to overwhip, as it can turn grainy.

Fill a piping bag fitted with a circular tip with the whipped chocolate Chantilly cream.

ASSEMBLE THE ÉCLAIRS

Slice the éclairs lengthwise. Fill another piping bag fitted with a ½-inch (12-mm) round tip with the Baileys milk chocolate mousse and generously pipe the mousse onto the éclairs.

Secure a chocolate disk atop each éclair with a dollop of mousse. (Don't be shy; we're building edible architecture here.) Pipe the whipped Chantilly over the chocolate disk, forming delicate mounds that rival clouds. Step back and admire your creation.

The éclairs are best enjoyed the day they're assembled, when the choux is still crisp and the fillings are freshly whipped. Once assembled, éclairs can be refrigerated (loosely covered) for up to 6 hours, but note that the choux will soften slightly.

Croissants are like love letters from the pastry gods, and today we're penning an epic romance. Layers upon layers, soft whispers of rosewater, and pistachios so indulgent they deserve their own fan club. Roll this dough right, and I promise you'll feel as buttered up as these beauties. These croissant wheels are irresistible: Make these and you'll have suitors banging down your door. Don't say I didn't warn you!

Pistachio Rosewater Croissant Wheels

MAKES 10 TO 12 CROISSANT WHEELS

FOR THE CROISSANT WHEELS

7 cups plus 2 tablespoons (980g) all-purpose flour

½ cup (100g) granulated sugar

2 teaspoons whole milk, plus 1 tablespoon for the egg wash

4 teaspoons fine sea salt

4 teaspoons instant dry yeast

¼ cup (55g) unsalted butter

1¾ cups (415ml) water

Two 8.8-ounce (250g) butter sheets OR 17.6 ounces (500g) unsalted European-style butter, softened (substitute Président unsalted butter or Vermont Creamery unsalted cultured butter, if desired)

1 egg for the egg wash

FOR THE PISTACHIO ROSEWATER PASTRY CREAM

2 cups (475ml) whole milk

½ cup (100g) superfine or caster sugar

⅓ cup (45g) cornstarch

4 egg yolks

1 teaspoon rosewater

⅓ cup (95g) pistachio paste

2 tablespoons unsalted butter

Edible rose petals for topping

½ cup (60g) chopped unsalted pistachios for topping

MAKE THE CROISSANT WHEELS

In the bowl of a stand mixer fitted with the dough hook, combine the flour, granulated sugar, 2 teaspoons of the milk, the sea salt, yeast, butter, and water. Mix on low speed until a shaggy dough forms, 2 to 3 minutes. Scrape down the sides. It's a seductive little start.

Increase the mixer speed to medium-high and knead the dough for 8 to 9 minutes. You're looking for dough that feels elastic but breaks a little during the windowpane test (see page 20)—like a shy flirtation.

Shape the dough into a ball, flatten it slightly, and wrap it in plastic wrap. Let it rest at room temperature for 2 hours (if your room temperature is between 66° and 70°F [19° and 21°C]; 60 to 75 minutes for warmer rooms). The dough should puff gently but not double in size. Chill the dough in the refrigerator for at least 30 minutes, until it is cold and firm to match the butter's firmness before laminating.

On a lightly floured surface, roll the chilled dough into a rectangle measuring 12 by 18 inches (30 by 45cm).

CONTINUED

Pistachio Rosewater Croissant Wheels

CONTINUED

Roll the butter between two sheets of parchment paper into a rectangle measuring 12 x 9 inches (30 by 23cm). Match the thickness to the dough's thickness for harmony. Place the butter rectangle in the center of the dough. Fold the long edges of the dough over to meet in the middle, encasing the butter snugly. Gently seal the seams with a rolling pin.

On the lightly floured surface, roll the dough toward the open edges to a thickness of ⅓ inch (8 to 9mm), keeping the shape rectangular. Allow it to rest briefly, like a well-earned sigh.

Fold the dough into thirds like a letter. Snip the folded edges lightly to prevent shrinkage. Wrap the dough in plastic wrap and refrigerate for 30 to 45 minutes. Repeat this rolling, folding, and chilling twice more, for a total of three folds.

Line a baking sheet with parchment paper. Roll the folded dough to a ¼-inch (6-mm) thickness. Cut the dough into strips about 3½ by 9 inches (9 by 23cm).

Roll each strip into a tight spiral (resembling a snail shape) and place the spirals on the prepared baking sheet, leaving enough space between each spiral for expansion during proofing. Let the spirals proof until they rise slightly, 1½ to 2 hours—just a gentle puff, not too much.

Preheat the oven to 375°F (190°C).

In a small bowl, mix together the egg and the remaining 1 tablespoon milk to make an egg wash. Brush the proofed dough with the egg wash for a golden glow.

Bake until puffed and golden, 20 to 25 minutes. Transfer them to a wire rack and cool completely before filling.

MAKE THE PISTACHIO ROSEWATER PASTRY CREAM

In a medium saucepan, heat the milk until it simmers—don't let it boil; we're simmering with anticipation.

In a separate bowl, whisk together the superfine sugar, cornstarch, and egg yolks until smooth and eager.

Gradually pour the hot milk into the egg yolk mixture, whisking to keep it together. Return the mixture to the saucepan. Heat over medium heat, stirring, until thickened and bubbling—this is when the magic happens. Remove from the heat.

Off heat, stir in the rosewater, pistachio paste, and butter until silky. Transfer the pastry cream to a clean, heatproof bowl and press plastic wrap directly onto the surface to prevent a skin forming. Chill until firm, about 2 hours.

ASSEMBLE THE PISTACHIO ROSEWATER CROISSANT WHEELS

Fill a piping bag fitted with a round tip and pipe the chilled cream into the centers of the cooled croissant wheels. Finish with a sprinkle of rose petals and crushed pistachios for an elegant crunch.

Crisp, caramelized puff pastry, silky salted caramel vanilla custard, and candied hazelnuts—this dessert doesn't just flirt, it full-on seduces. It's the kind of treat that looks innocent but has plans to ruin your diet, your self-control, and possibly your life (in the best way). Assemble this masterpiece and prepare for gasps, swoons, and people asking for your phone number . . . because a dessert like this deserves a second date.

Salted Caramel Vanilla Mille–Feuilles

MAKES 10 MILLE-FEUILLES

FOR THE PREPARED BUTTER

1⅔ cups (380g) unsalted butter

1 cup plus 3 tablespoons (165g) all-purpose flour

FOR THE DOUGH

2¾ cups (385g) all-purpose flour

2½ teaspoons kosher salt

½ cup (110g) unsalted butter

⅔ cup (160ml) water

1 teaspoon distilled white vinegar

2 tablespoons sugar

FOR THE SALTED CARAMEL VANILLA CUSTARD

2 cups (475ml) whole milk

¼ teaspoon vanilla bean paste

½ cup (100g) sugar

⅛ cup custard powder, such as Bird's Custard Powder

¾ cup (190g) egg yolks (from about 10 eggs)

½ cup (160g) salted caramel sauce, homemade (see page 211) or store-bought

½ cup plus 2 tablespoons (140g) unsalted butter, softened

Candied hazelnuts for garnish

Chocolate cigars for garnish

Candied sugar for garnish

MAKE THE PREPARED BUTTER

In the bowl of a stand mixer fitted with the paddle attachment, combine the butter and flour and mix on medium-low speed until a firm paste forms. Spread the mixture onto a guitar sheet (see page 18), cover with another guitar sheet, and roll into a square about 14 by 14 inches (36 by 36cm). Chill in the refrigerator for 30 to 45 minutes or until firm.

MAKE THE DOUGH

In the clean bowl of the stand mixer fitted with the dough hook, combine the flour, salt, butter, water, and vinegar and mix on medium speed until a smooth, elastic dough forms, about 20 minutes. Perform a windowpane test (see page 20) to check gluten development.

On a lightly floured surface, shape the dough into a 7 by 7-inch (18 by 18-cm) square, wrap it in plastic wrap, and chill in the refrigerator for 25 minutes.

CONTINUED

Salted Caramel Vanilla Mille–Feuilles

CONTINUED

Place the dough in the center of the butter square and fold the butter around the dough to form an envelope. Chill briefly (20 to 30 minutes) in the refrigerator.

Time to laminate. On a lightly floured surface, roll the dough into a rectangle approximately 24 by 10 inches (60 by 25cm). Perform a double turn: Fold both short edges into the center, then fold in half. Rest in the fridge for 20 to 30 minutes. Repeat the process two more times (three double turns total).

Preheat the oven to 375°F (190°C). Line a rimmed baking sheet with parchment paper and have another baking sheet on hand.

On a lightly floured surface, roll the rested pastry ⅛ inch (3mm) thick. Prick the pastry all over with a fork and sprinkle with the sugar. Gently roll the sugar into the dough.

Place the pastry on the prepared baking sheet and cover with another sheet of parchment paper. Weigh it down with the other baking sheet to ensure even caramelization. Bake for 10 minutes. Remove the top baking sheet and the parchment paper, then bake until caramelized and golden, another 7 to 8 minutes.

Let the baked pastry cool completely on the baking tray for about 15 minutes. Then transfer it to a cutting board and use a sharp knife to cut the pastry into 30 rectangles, each 4 by 1½ inches (10 by 4cm).

MAKE THE SALTED CARAMEL VANILLA CUSTARD

In a medium saucepan, combine the milk and vanilla paste and bring to a boil.

In a large bowl, whisk together the sugar, custard powder, and egg yolks until smooth.

Gradually pour the hot milk mixture into the egg yolk mixture, whisking continuously. Return the custard mixture to the saucepan. Cook over medium heat, whisking, until the mixture boils. Boil for 1 minute and remove from the heat.

Let the custard cool to 140°F (60°C). Whisk in the salted caramel sauce and softened butter until smooth. Strain the custard through a fine-mesh sieve into a bowl and cover with plastic wrap pressed directly onto the surface. Chill in the refrigerator for at least 1 hour.

ASSEMBLE THE SALTED CARAMEL VANILLA MILLE-FEUILLES

Fill a piping bag fitted with a ½-inch (12- or 13-mm) round tip with the salted caramel vanilla custard and pipe the custard onto one pastry rectangle. Top with another pastry layer and more custard. Finish with a final pastry rectangle. Repeat using the remaining rectangles and custard.

Decorate, please! Garnish with candied hazelnuts, chocolate cigars, or candied sugar.

Ah, the tarte tatin. Proof that even a kitchen disaster can turn into a culinary masterpiece. Legend has it that this dessert was born from a glorious whoopsie. But don't worry, we're skipping the chaos and heading straight for perfection. With spiced cider caramel so luxurious it should have its own bank account and with apples cuddled under golden puff pastry, this beauty is the ultimate showstopper. And hey, if you drop it during the flip, just call it "deconstructed." It's French, it's fancy, and no one will question it.

Apple Tarte Tatin

MAKES ONE 10-INCH (25-CM) TARTE TATIN, 8 TO 10 SERVINGS

FOR THE APPLE CIDER CARAMEL

2½ cups (590ml) unsweetened apple cider or fresh apple juice

1½ cups (300g) sugar

¼ cup plus 1½ tablespoons (80g) unsalted butter, cubed

2 teaspoons ground cinnamon

1 tablespoon pure vanilla extract or vanilla bean paste

FOR THE APPLES

6 to 8 medium apples (such as Gala, about 1½ pounds [750g]), peeled, cored, and quartered

Juice of 1 lemon

1¾ pounds (700g) high-quality store-bought puff pastry, thawed

Vanilla bean ice cream or crème fraîche for serving

MAKE THE APPLE CIDER CARAMEL

In a 10-inch (25-cm) ovenproof skillet or cast-iron pan, combine the apple cider and sugar and simmer gently over medium heat for 12 to 15 minutes, stirring occasionally, until the liquid reduces and turns a golden caramel color (293°F [145°C]). If using cast iron, keep the heat on the lower side of medium, as the pan's heat retention may cause the caramel to darken too quickly. Remove from the heat and stir in the butter, cinnamon, and vanilla until smooth. Let the bubbles subside. This is molten magic.

MAKE THE APPLES

In a large bowl, toss the apple quarters in the lemon juice to prevent browning. Think of it as a quick beauty spa for your fruit.

Arrange the apples in the warm caramel, rounded-side down, like laying out a fruit mosaic. Lower the heat to low and simmer until the apples soften slightly, shrink, and begin to absorb some of the caramel, 8 to 10 minutes. Fill any gaps with additional apple pieces for a snug, picture-perfect fit. Remove from the heat and let the contents rest until the caramel thickens slightly but is still warm and fluid, 5 to 10 minutes.

CONTINUED

Apple Tarte Tatin

CONTINUED

ASSEMBLE THE APPLE TARTE TATIN

Preheat the oven to 425°F (220°C).

On a lightly floured surface, roll out the puff pastry to ¼ inch (6mm) thick. Cut a pastry disk ¾ inch (2cm) larger than the pan with the apples. Prick the pastry all over with a fork to keep it from overpuffing. This isn't a balloon show!

Drape the pastry disk over the apples in the pan, gently tucking the edges into the pan like a cozy blanket. Place the pan on a baking sheet to catch caramel drips (trust me, your oven will thank you). Bake until the pastry is golden, puffed, and audibly calling your name, 18 to 20 minutes. Cool the tarte tatin in the pan for 10 minutes.

Invert the tarte tatin carefully onto a serving plate. It's a little acrobatic, but worth the applause. Serve warm with a decadent scoop of vanilla bean ice cream or a dollop of crème fraîche.

Oh, pumpkin spice, how you've taken over the world and, now, my kitchen. Pumpkin spice and I have a complicated relationship. Every fall, it tries to steal my thunder, but I remind it who the real star is: the Donut Daddy. Serving this pie might make just about anyone follow you home like a lovesick puppy. They'll claim it's the pumpkin spice, but let's be real—it's the naughty praline on top. And if you get caught eating the leftovers straight from the pan at midnight? That's just self-care.

Spiced Pumpkin Pie with Pecan Praline Topping

MAKES ONE 9-INCH (23-CM) PIE, 8 TO 10 SERVINGS

FOR THE PIECRUST

1¼ cups (175g) all-purpose flour

½ teaspoon kosher salt

½ cup (110g) cold unsalted butter, cubed

3 tablespoons cold water

FOR THE PUMPKIN FILLING

1¼ cups (300ml) heavy cream

1 cup (250g) pumpkin puree

2 eggs

½ cup (100g) packed light brown sugar

2 tablespoons granulated sugar

1½ teaspoons ground cinnamon

½ teaspoon ground ginger

¼ teaspoon ground nutmeg

Pinch of ground cloves

½ teaspoon kosher salt

FOR THE PECAN PRALINE TOPPING

1 cup (120g) pecans, roughly chopped

½ cup (100g) granulated sugar

¼ cup (60ml) heavy cream

2 tablespoons unsalted butter

Pinch of kosher salt

Whipped cream or vanilla ice cream for serving (optional)

MAKE THE PIECRUST

In a large bowl, combine the flour and salt. Add the cubed butter and rub it into the flour with your fingertips until it resembles coarse crumbs. Alternatively, you can mix in a stand mixer with the paddle attachment on low speed until the mixture resembles coarse crumbs, 2 to 3 minutes. Work quickly as this is a no-sweat zone.

Gradually add the cold water, 1 tablespoon at a time, mixing gently until the dough comes together (or you can use the stand mixer on low speed until the dough comes together, about 1 minute). Shape the dough into a ball, flatten it into a disk, and wrap it tightly in plastic wrap to prevent drying. Chill in the refrigerator for at least 30 minutes.

Preheat the oven to 400°F (200°C).

CONTINUED

Spiced Pumpkin Pie with Pecan Praline Topping

CONTINUED

On a lightly floured surface, roll out the chilled dough to fit into a 9-inch (23-cm) pie plate. Place the dough into the bottom and sides of the plate. Trim the edges and crimp them like the fancy pastry artist you are.

Line the crust with parchment paper and layer with pie weights because, yes, even pastry needs a gym session. Bake for 15 minutes, then carefully remove the weights and the parchment paper. Return the crust to the oven and bake until lightly golden, an additional 5 minutes.

MAKE THE PUMPKIN FILLING

In the bowl of a stand mixer fitted with the whisk attachment, combine the cream, pumpkin puree, eggs, brown sugar, granulated sugar, cinnamon, ginger, nutmeg, cloves, and salt. Mix on medium speed until smooth and well combined, 2 minutes. Pour the luscious mixture into the prebaked crust.

Lower the oven temperature to 350°F (175°C). Bake until the filling is set but still slightly jiggly in the center, 35 to 40 minutes. (A little wiggle is part of its charm.) Let the pie cool completely on a wire rack. It's hard, but patience is part of the pie game. While the pie cools, make the praline topping.

MAKE THE PECAN PRALINE TOPPING

In a small saucepan, combine the pecans, granulated sugar, cream, and butter over medium heat, stirring continuously, coaxing the mixture into a thick, caramelized topping, 5 to 7 minutes. Remove from the heat and stir in the salt, because sweet and salty is always a winning combo.

ASSEMBLE THE SPICED PUMPKIN PIE WITH PECAN PRALINE TOPPING

Spoon the warm pecan praline topping evenly over the cooled pie, spreading it like a delicious secret you can't keep. Let it set for 15 minutes before slicing.

Serve with whipped cream or a scoop of vanilla ice cream (if using), because life's too short for plain pie.

They say tying a cherry stem in a knot with your tongue is the ultimate party trick. Well, Donut Daddy's been there, done that, and upgraded the game. These Cherry Petits Gâteaux are the real showstoppers: luscious cherry jelly, decadent chocolate mousse, and a tart shell so buttery, it might make you blush. Serve these at your next gathering, and your guests will be too busy swooning to notice your cherry-stem skills or lack thereof.

For this recipe you'll need: eight individual tart pans, about 3 inches (7.5cm) in diameter for the tart bases; eight small-cavity molds, about 1½ inches (4cm) in diameter, for the chocolate mousse; eight circular molds, 1¼ to 1½ inches (3 to 4cm) in diameter, for the cherry jelly inserts.

Each component requires careful layering, but the final result is worth every step. Now let's get started!

Cherry Petits Gâteaux

MAKES 8 SMALL TARTS

FOR THE CHERRY JELLY INSERTS

½ teaspoon gelatin powder

2 teaspoons cold water

3 tablespoons granulated sugar

½ teaspoon pectin NH (see page 21)

¾ cup (120g) cherries or sour cherries

¼ cup (48g) cherry puree

FOR THE CHOCOLATE HAZELNUT TART BASES

1¾ cups (245g) all-purpose flour

⅓ cup (40g) confectioners' sugar

3 tablespoons unsweetened Dutch-processed cocoa powder

¼ cup plus 3 tablespoons (100g) cold unsalted butter, cubed

1 egg yolk

1 to 2 tablespoons cold water

FOR THE CRUSHED ALMOND AND CHOCOLATE GANACHE FILLING

⅔ cup (160ml) heavy cream

7 ounces (200g) dark chocolate (70% to 75%), chopped

5 teaspoons black raspberry liqueur (such as Chambord)

⅓ cup (40g) chopped roasted almonds

3 cups (720ml) Basic Chocolate Mousse (see page 204)

FOR THE MILK CHOCOLATE STEMS

5 ounces (140g) milk chocolate, finely chopped

Drops of green oil-based food coloring

1½ cups (360ml) cups Mirror Glaze (page 207), before the glaze cools

Pinch of red food dye (such as beet juice powder or Red 40)

CONTINUED

Cherry Petits Gâteaux

CONTINUED

MAKE THE CHERRY JELLY INSERTS

In a small bowl, combine the gelatin and cold water and let it sit for 5 minutes to bloom.

In a separate small bowl, combine the granulated sugar and pectin NH.

Then in a medium saucepan, combine the cherries and cherry puree and warm gently over medium-low heat. Stir in the sugar mixture, bring to a boil, and cook for 2 minutes. Remove from the heat and add the bloomed gelatin.

Pour into eight 1¼- to 1½-inch (3- to 4-cm) circular molds. Freeze until solid.

MAKE THE CHOCOLATE HAZELNUT TART BASE

In a large bowl, combine the flour, confectioners' sugar, and cocoa powder. Rub in the cubed butter using your fingertips or a bench scraper until it resembles coarse crumbs. Add the egg yolk and 1 tablespoon cold water. Mix gently until the dough comes together, adding more water as needed. Shape the dough into a flat disk. Place it on a lightly floured surface. Wrap it tightly in plastic wrap and chill in the refrigerator for at least 30 minutes.

Preheat the oven to 350°F (175°C). Have ready eight 3-inch (7.5-cm) tart pans for the tart bases.

Roll out the chilled dough to ⅛ inch (3mm) thick. Cut circles slightly larger than the tart pans and press the circles into the pans. Trim the edges neatly. Prick the bases all over with a fork, line the tart pans with parchment paper, and fill each tart pan with pie weights.

Bake for 15 minutes. Remove the weights and parchment paper and bake until the tart is dry to the touch and just starting to darken slightly, another 5 to 8 minutes. Cool completely in the tart pans on wire racks before filling.

MAKE THE CRUSHED ALMOND AND CHOCOLATE GANACHE FILLING

In a small saucepan, heat the cream until it begins to simmer.

In a heatproof bowl, add the chopped dark chocolate and pour the hot cream over the chocolate. Let sit for 1 to 2 minutes, then whisk until smooth. Stir in the black raspberry liqueur.

Sprinkle some of the crushed almonds into each tart shell, then pour the prepared chocolate ganache into the tart shells, filling them halfway. Chill in the refrigerator until firm, at least 30 minutes.

START THE GREAT ASSEMBLY

Pour the chocolate mousse into eight 1½-inch-cavity molds. Insert a frozen cherry jelly ball in each, ensuring full coverage. Smooth the surface and freeze for at least 4 hours, or until fully set. They will keep in the freezer for up to 1 week if stored in an airtight container.

MAKE THE MILK CHOCOLATE STEMS

In a food processor, combine the chopped milk chocolate and green food coloring and pulse until the mixture is pliable. Roll portions of the mixture into thin stems and trim to your desired length. Cool in the refrigerator until the chocolate stems are firm enough to hold their shape, 10 to 15 minutes

ASSEMBLE THE CHERRY PETITS GÂTEAUX

In a mixing bowl, use an immersion blender to blend the warm mirror glaze and red dye until smooth and fully combined.

Remove the frozen mousse molds from the freezer and remove the molds themselves. Glaze with mirror glaze by placing the frozen mousse balls on a wire rack set over a sheet of wax paper to catch drips. Pour the glaze evenly over each mousse ball, letting the excess drip off naturally. If needed, use an offset spatula to gently smooth out any uneven areas. Once the glaze has set slightly, carefully transfer each glazed mousse ball onto a ganache-filled tart shell. Add chocolate stems for a final touch.

Serve each Cherry Petite Gâteau on an individual dessert plate for an elegant presentation. Allow the gateaux to sit at room temperature for 5 to 7 minutes before serving to slightly soften the mousse without losing structure.

Let me just say this up front: This cheesecake should probably be illegal. Like, someone might call the dessert police when you serve it. It's so rich, so decadent, so downright scandalous that you'll feel like you're smuggling forbidden indulgence across some international border. I mean, a hazelnut shortbread base? Layers of white and dark chocolate crémeux? Now, about that crémeux—French for "creamy"—it's silkier than mousse but lighter than pudding, striking the perfect balance between richness and elegance. Strawberries, roasted hazelnuts, and gold leaf? If desserts had a black market, this one would be at the top of the list, sold in whispers by someone in a trench coat.

Chocolate Cheesecake Seduction

MAKES 8 TO 10 SERVINGS

FOR THE WHITE CHOCOLATE CRÉMEUX

1½ sheets (3.75g) platinum gelatin

1 cup (240ml) whole milk

1 cup (240ml) heavy cream

6 egg yolks

3 tablespoons superfine or caster sugar

12½ ounces (355g) high-quality white chocolate, chopped

FOR THE DARK CHOCOLATE CRÉMEUX

1⅛ cups (270ml) heavy cream

4 egg yolks

2½ tablespoons superfine or caster sugar

3½ ounces (100g) couverture milk chocolate

5 ounces (145g) couverture dark chocolate

FOR THE HAZELNUT SHORTBREAD BASE

½ cup (110g) unsalted butter, cubed, plus 3½ tablespoons, melted

½ teaspoon kosher salt

¼ cup (50g) granulated sugar

1¼ cups (175g) all-purpose flour

½ cup (70g) finely crushed roasted hazelnuts

FOR THE CHEESECAKE FILLING

12 ounces (340g) cream cheese, softened

½ cup (100g) granulated sugar

2 eggs, whisked

2 tablespoons heavy cream

5¼ ounces (150g) dark chocolate (75%), melted

2½ tablespoons Dutch-processed cocoa powder

Warmed Nutella for spreading

3½ ounces (100g) finely crushed roasted hazelnuts for topping (optional)

14 medium fresh strawberries for topping

1 packet (3⅜-inch [85-mm] square) edible gold leaf for topping (optional)

MAKE THE WHITE CHOCOLATE CRÉMEUX

In a small bowl, soak the gelatin sheet in cold water for about 5 minutes until softened. Squeeze out excess water and set aside.

CONTINUED

Chocolate Cheesecake Seduction

CONTINUED

In a small saucepan, heat the milk and cream over medium heat until steaming but not boiling.

In a large bowl, combine the egg yolks and superfine sugar and whisk together until they're pale and dreamy. Slowly pour the warm milk mixture into the egg yolk mixture while whisking, tempering it with care (like a gentle love letter, not a frantic DM). Return the mixture to the saucepan and cook over low heat, stirring continuously, until it thickens and its temperature reaches 179° to 185°F (82° to 85°C).

Into a large bowl with the chopped white chocolate, strain the warm mixture over the white chocolate and add the softened gelatin. Whisk until the cream is as smooth as a slow jazz track. Chill in the fridge overnight.

MAKE THE DARK CHOCOLATE CRÉMEUX

In a small saucepan, heat the cream until steaming but not boiling. In a large bowl, combine the egg yolks and superfine sugar and whisk together until they're pale and dreamy. Slowly pour the warm cream into the egg yolk mixture while whisking, tempering it with care. Return the mixture to the saucepan and cook over low heat, stirring continuously, until it thickens and its temperature reaches 179° to 185°F (82° to 85°C). Pour the mixture over both the milk and dark chocolates in a bowl. Whisk until it's glossy and sinful. Chill in the fridge overnight.

MAKE THE HAZELNUT SHORTBREAD BASE

Preheat the oven to 350°F (175°C).

In a large bowl, combine the cubed butter, salt, and granulated sugar and cream together with a wooden spoon or silicone spatula until smooth. Stir in the flour and hazelnuts until the dough just comes together. It should look like it's trying not to fall apart, but in a sexy way.

Line a baking sheet with parchment paper. Press the dough onto the prepared baking sheet, spreading it into an even layer about ¼ inch (6mm) thick and bake until golden and fragrant, 15 to 20 minutes. Let it cool completely on the pan. Once cooled, process it in a food processor until finely ground. Transfer to a bowl and add the melted butter and mix by hand with a wooden spoon until it's like damp sand that holds together when pressed.

Grab a 9-inch (23-cm) circular or heart-shaped springform pan. Line the base with parchment paper and press the crumbs down into a layer that is ⅛-inch (2 to 3mm) thick, smoothing it with the back of a spoon. Set aside.

MAKE THE CHEESECAKE FILLING

Preheat the oven to 325°F (165°C).

In a large bowl, combine the cream cheese and granulated sugar and cream together until smooth (no lumps, no drama). Gradually add the whisked eggs, stirring continuously. Stir in the cream, followed by the melted dark chocolate and cocoa powder. Pour the mixture over the prepared shortbread base in the springform pan, filling it three-quarters of the way.

Bake until the edges are set and the center has a slight jiggle, 50 to 55 minutes. Turn off the oven and let the cheesecake rest inside for 15 minutes, like it's cooling off after an epic performance. Then place the cheesecake (still in the pan) on a wire rack and let it cool completely. Cover the pan with plastic wrap then chill in the refrigerator overnight. Yes, another overnight step.

ASSEMBLE THE CHOCOLATE CHEESECAKE SEDUCTION

Before assembling, release the sides of the springform pan and carefully transfer the cheesecake to a serving plate or cake stand.

With a whisk, whip the white chocolate crémeux and the dark chocolate crémeux separately until they're just shy of firm peaks. Be gentle—nobody likes an overwhipped crémeux. Fill a piping bag fitted with a ⅓-inch (8-mm) circular tip with the white chocolate crémeux. Fill another piping bag fitted with a ⅓-inch (8-mm) circular tip with the dark chocolate crémeux.

Spread a thin layer of the warmed Nutella over the top of the cheesecake, then sprinkle the top generously with the crushed hazelnuts. This is where things get dangerously good.

Start piping from the outer edge—first using the dark chocolate crémeux, then the white chocolate crémeux, and finishing with a strawberry—working your way inward in concentric circles.

Finish by delicately placing pieces of gold leaf on different parts of the creams. The gold leaf is unnecessary, extravagant, and completely fabulous. Slice the cheesecake with a hot, clean knife for smooth cuts. Wipe the knife between slices for the best presentation.

04

Breakfast in Bed

Quick-and-Easy Recipes to Savor Between the Sheets

Good morning, darling. Picture this: Sunlight streaming through the curtains, the scent of cinnamon buns wafting through the air, and a tray of desserts so luscious, it feels like the Donut Daddy himself has come by to personally deliver a little slice of heaven.

This chapter is all about awakening your senses. The smell of freshly baked banana bread and pear muffins, the silky touch of mascarpone cream on French toast, and the sound of someone whispering, "Wow, you really made this?" over a bowl of chocolate cherry rice pudding. These breakfasts are the gateway to morning ecstasy.

These recipes are truly transformative: A plate of double chocolate waffles with burnt vanilla ice cream could turn a sleepy "good morning" into an all-day event. That fruit salad? It's not just refreshing, it's the kind of thing that makes you think, "I should probably cancel my plans today."

So fluff those pillows, cue up some sultry music, and let Donut Daddy take care of your mornings.

Sweetheart, let's have a breakfast love affair. Juicy apples, buttery streusel, and a cinnamon swirl so decadent it could teach romance novels a thing or two. This cake doesn't just go with coffee; it might make you forget coffee altogether. But fair warning: Once you pull this beauty out of the oven, don't expect anyone to leave your kitchen—or your heart.

Apples, Streusel, and Cinnamon Swirls of Desire

MAKES ONE 8-INCH (20-CM) CAKE, 8 TO 10 SERVINGS

FOR THE CINNAMON SWIRL

½ cup (100g) packed dark brown sugar

2 teaspoons ground cinnamon

3 tablespoons unsalted butter, melted

FOR THE STREUSEL TOPPING

¾ cup (105g) all-purpose flour

½ cup (100g) packed dark brown sugar

⅓ cup (75g) unsalted butter, softened

1 teaspoon ground cinnamon

¼ cup (30g) chopped pecans (optional)

FOR THE CAKE

2 cups (280g) all-purpose flour

¾ cup (150g) granulated sugar

2 teaspoons baking powder

½ teaspoon kosher salt

1 teaspoon ground cinnamon

½ cup (110g) unsalted butter, softened

2 eggs

¾ cup (175ml) whole milk or buttermilk

1½ teaspoons pure vanilla extract

2 medium apples (such as Gala), peeled, cored, and diced

Whipped cream for garnish

Caramel sauce, homemade (see page 211) or store-bought, for garnish

Preheat the oven to 350°F (175°C). Grease an 8-inch (20-cm) springform pan and line it with parchment paper for easy release. This will help preserve the delicate streusel topping when removing the cake from the pan.

MAKE THE CINNAMON SWIRL

In a small bowl, combine the brown sugar, cinnamon, and melted butter and mix until smooth and luxurious. Set aside.

MAKE THE STREUSEL TOPPING

In a large bowl, combine the flour, brown sugar, softened butter, cinnamon, and pecans (if using). Use your fingertips to create a crumbly texture. Think "buttery clouds of perfection." Set aside.

CONTINUED

Apples, Streusel, and Cinnamon Swirls of Desire

CONTINUED

MAKE THE CAKE BATTER

In the bowl of a stand mixer fitted with the paddle attachment, combine the flour, granulated sugar, baking powder, salt, and cinnamon and mix on medium speed. Add the softened butter, eggs, milk, and vanilla and mix until smooth and slightly thick, 2 to 3 minutes. Gently fold in the diced apples with a spatula, spreading the fruity love evenly.

ASSEMBLE THE APPLES, STREUSEL, AND CINNAMON SWIRLS OF DESIRE

Pour half the batter into the prepared pan and spread evenly. Drizzle the cinnamon swirl mixture over the batter in an artful spiral. Cover with the remaining batter, smoothing the top gently. Sprinkle the streusel topping generously over the surface, making sure every bite gets its share of crunch.

Bake until a toothpick inserted into the center comes out clean, 45 to 50 minutes. The cake should be tender, moist, and crowned with a golden, crunchy topping. Let the cake cool in the pan for 10 to 15 minutes, then transfer to a wire rack to cool further.

Serve warm or at room temperature with a dollop of whipped cream or a drizzle of caramel sauce. Bonus points if you eat it in bed.

Silky, creamy, and bursting with berries, this tasty bowl is thick enough to hold your spoon but smooth enough to make you question why you ever settled for plain yogurt. How about the toppings? They're like the accessories on a perfectly tailored outfit: granola for crunch, coconut for sass, and that walnut or macadamia nut butter drizzle? Let's just say it's the drop-everything-and-indulge moment.

Blueberry Bliss Bowl

MAKES 1 LARGE OR 2 SMALL SERVINGS

FOR THE BLUEBERRY BLISS

1½ cups (210g) frozen blueberries

1 large frozen banana

½ cup (70g) frozen mixed berries

½ cup (120ml) unsweetened almond milk, or more if needed

2 teaspoons honey

FOR THE TOPPINGS

¼ cup (25g) granola, homemade (see page 183) or store-bought

¼ cup (35g) sliced fresh strawberries

½ fresh kiwi (40g), sliced

1 tablespoon shredded unsweetened coconut

1 teaspoon chia seeds

1 tablespoon walnut or macadamia nut butter

1 tablespoon (10g) chopped unsalted pistachios

MAKE THE BLUEBERRY BLISS

Let the frozen blueberries, banana, and mixed berries thaw slightly—just enough to make your blender purr instead of struggle.

In the jar of a blender, combine the slightly thawed blueberries, banana, mixed berries, almond milk, and honey. Starting on low speed and gradually increasing to high, blend until smooth and creamy, like the dessert equivalent of a stolen kiss. Adjust the consistency with a splash of almond milk if needed, but remember, you want it thick enough to spoon, not sip.

ASSEMBLE THE BLUEBERRY BLISS BOWL

Pour the luscious blueberry mixture into your serving bowl (or bowls), smoothing the top with the back of your spoon like a master artist at work. Arrange the toppings in sections or swirls: granola, fresh strawberries, kiwi slices, shredded coconut, and chia seeds. Think of it as decorating a love letter to yourself. Finish with a drizzle of nut butter and a sprinkle of pistachios.

Serve immediately before the masterpiece melts. If anyone asks why you're grinning, just tell them it's the berries.

These bars are like a perfect first date—sweet, a little nutty, and leaving you wanting more. Soft and chewy with just the right amount of crunch, they've got enough wholesome charm to meet your parents, but enough chocolaty decadence to make you blush. Oh, and they're gluten-free and protein-packed, so you can totally pretend they're a health food while sneaking a second . . . or third. These bars don't just fuel your day—they flirt with it.

GLUTEN-FREE OPTION

Love You Oat–ways Bars

MAKES 9 TO 12 BARS

1½ cups (150g) old-fashioned oats (certified gluten-free)

½ cup (70g) rice flour

½ cup (100g) packed dark brown sugar

¼ cup (30g) protein powder (vanilla or unflavored)

½ teaspoon baking powder (gluten-free)

¼ teaspoon kosher salt

1 teaspoon ground cinnamon

½ cup (110g) unsalted butter, melted

2 tablespoons honey

1 egg

1 teaspoon pure vanilla extract

½ cup (70g) dried cranberries

½ cup (90g) dark chocolate chips

¼ cup (30g) chopped pecans (optional)

Preheat the oven to 350°F (175°C). Line an 8-inch (20-cm) square baking pan with parchment paper, leaving an overhang for easy removal.

In a large mixing bowl, combine the oats, rice flour, brown sugar, protein powder, baking powder, salt, and cinnamon and whisk together. It's like the dry team gearing up for the big game.

In a separate bowl, combine the melted butter, honey, egg, and vanilla and stir together until smooth and glossy. Think of it as the team pep talk—this is the moment where everything comes together.

Pour the butter mixture into the oat mixture, stirring until fully combined. Fold in the dried cranberries, dark chocolate chips, and pecans (if using). Every fold is like adding a little more love to the mix.

Spread the mixture evenly into the prepared baking pan. Press it down gently with a spatula—it's all about keeping things compact and cozy. Bake until the edges are golden brown and your kitchen smells like a hug, 20 to 25 minutes.

Let the bars cool in the pan for 10 minutes. Use the parchment overhang to lift them out gently. Slice into squares or rectangles (or triangles if you're feeling wild) and try not to eat them all at once.

These pancakes are a one-way ticket to breakfast paradise. With creamy ricotta and a hint of lemon zest, they're so light they might just float off your plate. Add a drizzle of syrup or a mountain of berries, and suddenly, every other pancake you've ever had feels like a distant memory.

But fair warning: Side effects may include uncontrollable moaning (it's the pancakes, promise), spontaneous marriage proposals from unsuspecting diners, and the realization that you've accidentally eaten ten without sharing. Don't blame yourself; these pancakes are irresistible.

Cloud Nine Ricotta Pancakes

MAKES 12 TO 15 PANCAKES

3 cups (420g) all-purpose flour

¼ cup plus 2 tablespoons (75g) sugar

1 tablespoon baking powder

¾ teaspoon kosher salt

1 tablespoon freshly grated lemon zest (optional)

2¼ cups (540g) ricotta cheese

1½ cups (360ml) buttermilk or whole milk

6 egg yolks

1 tablespoon pure vanilla extract

9 egg whites

Honey butter, fresh berries, maple syrup, mascarpone cream (see page 205), and/or caramelized fruit for topping (optional)

In a large mixing bowl, combine the flour, sugar, baking powder, salt, and lemon zest (if using) and whisk together.

In another bowl, combine the ricotta, buttermilk, egg yolks, and vanilla and mix until smooth. Stir slowly, as this is where the creamy miracle begins.

In the bowl of a stand mixer fitted with the whisk attachment, whip the egg whites, starting at low speed and gradually increasing to high until stiff peaks form, 4 to 5 minutes. The peaks should be glossy and elegant, like the perfect accessory to your batter.

Pour the ricotta mixture into the flour mixture and stir gently until just combined. Don't overmix; we want fluffy, not flat. Gently fold in the whipped egg whites in batches. This is where the batter gets its airy personality.

Heat a nonstick skillet or griddle over medium heat. Grease the warming pan lightly with butter. Working in batches if necessary, scoop ¼ cup of the batter for each pancake onto the warm skillet. Cook until bubbles form on the surface of the pancakes and their edges look set, 2 to 3 minutes. Flip the pancakes carefully and cook until golden brown, another 1 to 2 minutes. Each pancake should be as soft as your sweetest daydream.

Serve warm with your favorite toppings (if using): honey butter, berries, syrup, mascarpone cream, and/or caramelized fruit.

If you thought fruit salad was boring, think again. This is a flirtatious little number drizzled with a honey-lime glaze that's tangy, sweet, and downright irresistible. It's the perfect way to start your morning with a zing, whether you're serving it to someone special or treating yourself.

And those pomegranate arils? They may bring you spontaneous happiness, bursts of energy, and the sudden urge to book a tropical vacation.

Tropical Tease Fruit Salad

MAKES 2 TO 4 SERVINGS

FOR THE FRUIT SALAD

1 cup (150g) cubed fresh pineapple

1 cup (170g) cubed fresh mango

Segments from 1 large orange

¼ cup (60g) passion fruit pulp (from 2 fruits)

¼ cup (40g) fresh pomegranate arils

FOR THE HONEY-LIME GLAZE

1 teaspoon freshly grated lime zest

1 tablespoon freshly squeezed lime juice

1 tablespoon honey

Pinch of kosher salt

Fresh mint leaves for garnish (optional)

MAKE THE FRUIT SALAD

In a large mixing bowl, combine the pineapple, mango, and orange segments and stir together. Mix in the passion fruit pulp and pomegranate arils for a colorful pop.

MAKE THE HONEY-LIME GLAZE

In a small bowl, combine the lime zest, lime juice, honey, and salt and whisk together until smooth and glossy. The glaze should look like sunshine in a bowl.

ASSEMBLE THE TROPICAL TEASE FRUIT SALAD

Drizzle the honey-lime glaze over the fruit salad and toss gently to coat everything evenly. Don't rush it; let the fruits get properly acquainted.

Gently transfer the fruit salad to a serving bowl or divide it into two indulgent portions—or four if you're feeling generous. Scatter fresh mint leaves (if using) over the salad for a burst of herbal freshness and that gorgeous green garnish.